Pub Walks in Nottinghamshire

Abigail Bristow • Norman James
Chris Robson • Martin Smith

Published by Sigma Leisure – an imprint of
Sigma Press, 1 South Oak Lane, Wilmslow, Cheshire SK9 6AR, England.

British Library Cataloguing in Publication Data
A CIP record for this book is available from the British Library.

ISBN: 1-85058-349-8

Typesetting and Design by: Sigma Press, Wilmslow, Cheshire.

Maps by: Pam Upchurch

Text photographs: Chris Rushton and the authors

Cover photograph: Chris Rushton

Printed by: Manchester Free Press

General Disclaimer

Whilst every effort has been made to ensure that the information given in this book is correct, neither the publisher nor the author accept any responsibility for any inaccuracy.

Foreword

Nottinghamshire is without doubt rich in history, a history which is known internationally thanks to the legend and lore of Robin Hood. The county also has a varied and gentle landscape. Admittedly there are no hills of consequence and those seeking climbs and moorlands will travel to the neighbouring Peak District. There are, however, tracts of wild woodland, gentle valleys, and winding paths leading to some of the loveliest villages in the land.

The English village with parish church, post office and pub often makes a walk. What better feeling than to ramble a few miles before taking refreshment at the village local? Over the years, The Campaign For Real Ale, CAMRA, has championed the cause of those seeking choice of beers and in particular, real ale. The very same argument of choice applies to our pubs. Many date back to late medieval times, some were built to quench the thirst of weary travellers on coaching routes and others to serve the needs of the Victorian labourer working the land.

The character of each particular public house varies enormously. Some still retain a public bar for locals and walkers who are calling in for a pint, a game of darts or dominoes. Others have been "modernised" into one large lounge room, the emphasis being as much on the serving of food as good beer. The main issue, however, is choice. There needs to a be mix of pubs to suit all tastes. Pause a moment to reflect on what is taking place within the industry.

Recent Government measures to secure more choice at the bar by releasing a pub from the strong grip of the old tied house system has gone sadly wrong. The Big Brewers have relinquished hundreds of pubs in order to comply with the regulations but at the same time have resisted selling to existing tenants, many of whom have served them and local customers loyally over the years. Instead, the brewers have sought deals with new "retailing" companies buying up groups of pubs. In reality, the drinker has been faced with rising prices as a result of the process. At the same time, the push to fill the supermarket shelves with canned beer has continued unabated. These trends threaten the very existence of the country pub.

This book is very timely. It encourages those who seek the Great Outdoors to enjoy very pleasant countryside close to home, many of the walks being only a short bus or train ride away. The book also encourages the walker to give something back to the host rural community by calling in at the village local. The choice of pubs on the thirty walks introduces beers from a wide range of breweries including Batemans of Wainfleet, known to favour the retention of country pubs even if they are not as commercially viable as many of the Big Breweries now insist. The book also includes several pubs which sell brews from the independent Hardys and Hansons brewery and from the Mansfield Brewery.

Your enjoyment of these rural hostelries will help to maintain what could fast become an endangered species. Long live the tradition of the welcoming country pub.

Enjoy your walking and the pint afterwards !

Andrew Ludlow

CAMRA, Nottingham

Andrew Ludlow – pulling a pint of Nottinghamshire's Real Ale

The Oldest Inn in Nottinghamshire – and England!
(By permission, Nottingham City Council)

CONTENTS

THE WALKS

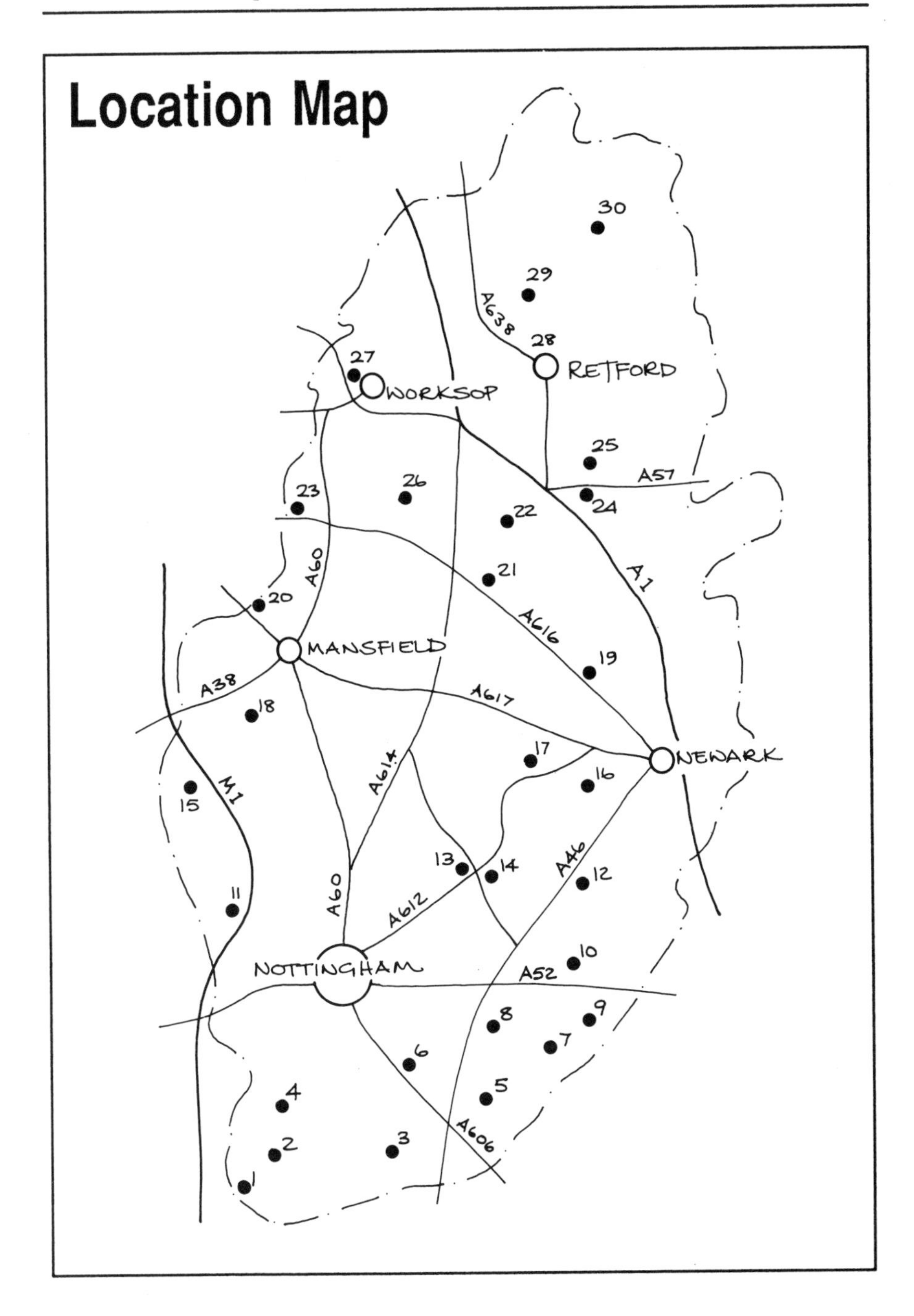
Location Map
WORKSOP
RETFORD
MANSFIELD
NEWARK
NOTTINGHAM
A638
A57
A1
A60
A616
A38
A617
A614
M1
A46
A612
A52
A606
1
2
3
4
5
6
7
8
9
10
11
12
13
14
15
16
17
18
19
20
21
22
23
24
25
26
27
28
29
30

INTRODUCTION

Geology

A county is shaped by its geology, and in Nottinghamshire that means large tracts of sandstone and marl. The yellow-brown Bunter sandstone covers about a third of the county, and is responsible for many famous landmarks. Its poor, acid soil has until recently been of little use for agriculture, and thus the covering of trees known as Sherwood Forest was left largely untouched. You only need to walk in the present woodlands after a dry spell to appreciate just how sandy the soil is. Occasionally the sandstone presents interesting surface formations, such as the Hemlock Stone at Bramcote, and it has been extensively hollowed out to produce the cave systems in Nottingham. Beneath lies the coal that is responsible for the development of many mining estates throughout the shire, often attached to old villages.

To the east, the clays and marls have produced a fertile land. They are also extremely suitable for making bricks and the distinctive red coloured pantile roofs of the villages. The north of the county used to be mainly marshland due to its proximity to sea level, but its drainage in the 17th century by the Dutch engineer Vermuyden partially alleviated the flooding. The gravel pits and rich farmland are a testimony to the alluvial material deposited there long ago.

Ice Age

The south was the only area affected by the Ice Age, and the gently undulating landscape has a heavy boulder clay soil as a legacy. Slicing its way through the south and east is the River Trent, so important in moulding the history of the area.

History

Creswell Crags on the north western corner has given us evidence of human occupation as long ago as 40,000 B.C., and the Trent valley has yielded a variety of flint implements and Bronze Age oak canoes. Some Iron Age hill forts may have existed in the Farnsfield area, but archaeological evidence is inconclusive.

Cola

The Romans established a road network throughout the county, with the Fosse Way and Ermine Street the best known. The presence of the Anglo-Saxon place name endings of *-ing, -ham, -ton* and *-worth* in many Trent Valley villages shows how important the navigable river was to them. Incidentally, Collingham means 'Home of the people of Cola' which perhaps suggests the origin of soft drinks.

Snot

The Danish influence is more felt the further north that you get, with the *-thwaite, -by* and *-thorpe* villages. When the Danes invaded the old Northumbrian kingdom and marched south in 867 their winter resting place was the then Mercian town of Snotengaham, the town of Snot, an Anglo-Saxon chief of the 6th century. No prizes for guessing that this is now Nottingham. Eventually Notts was divided up into eight territories or *wapentakes,* the names of which were mainly used in the 1974 local government reorganisation; Broxtowe, Bassetlaw and Rushcliffe stem from these times.

For the next 200 years, Nottinghamshire belonged at various times to the new English Kings and the Danes. The importance of Nottingham grew because it was at the head of the navigable Trent, it possessed the last bridge across the river before its mouth, and it was on one of the two roads from London to York.

Norman Conquest

After the Norman Conquest, motte and bailey castles were raised to maintain order. Grassy mounds at Laxton, Egmonton and Bothamstall among others mark their original sites. The great stone religious building began: Southwell Minster and the priories of Worksop, Blyth and Lenton. Newark and Nottingham Castles were begun, with Newark's prosperity assured by the diversion of the Fosse Way road through it in 1135. This eventually became part of the Great North Road, the precursor of the A1. Nottingham itself was really two towns: the Norman, centred on the new castle, and the Saxon clustered around St. Mary's church. This is why the present-day Sheriff carries two maces at ceremonial processions.

Sherwood Forest

'Forest' was an administrative term for hunting ground, and the "Shire-Wood" Forest was one of 90 such Royal Forests that covered about thirty-five percent of 13th century England. The forest encompassed scrubby heathland, farmland, villages and clearings as well as the Oak and Birch trees. There were strict laws administered by courts. Locals could not hunt or kill deer, fell trees, cut off branches, carry bow and arrow, make a clearing or erect a building without permission of the King or Chief Forester. Dogs had to have 3 claws removed from their front paws to stop them chasing deer. Exemptions to these laws were granted to powerful subjects, for example Bishops, and minor dignitaries such as Burgesses could hunt small game, including foxes and hares. In this environment it is easy to see how Robin Hood would be a local hero and how his legend would grow.

Robin Hood

On pain of persecution by the Tourist Board, we have to admit that he didn't really exist. However, as a symbol of the plight of the ordinary human in the 13th century he is important. Stories started towards the end of the 14th century of Robyn Hode, which was a common name, robbing the rich and helping the poor. Almost certainly a composite of several outlaws, time has exaggerated and embellished the original tales. Little John appears early on, but Friar Tuck and Maid Marian are 16th century inventions. The King referred to was originally one of the Edwards, and the title of Sheriff of Nottingham did not even exist until 1449. Later ballads moved Robin back in time to the 12th century, and Prince John made an appropriate baddie as foil to good King Richard. Still, it makes a good tale and does no harm to the local economy.

The Robin Hood Statue (Courtesy of Nottingham City Council)

Dissolution

Gradually the forest laws were relaxed and eventually the whole nature of the county was to change. The dissolution of the monasteries in the 1530s vested the estates to the Crown, and vast tracts of land were sold off or given mainly to local landowners. Thus in 1540 Sir John Byron bought Newstead Abbey and surrounding lands for £810, demolishing much of the church and adapting the remains of the priory as a house. Welbeck Abbey was granted to Richard Whalley, but eventually passed on to Bess of Hardwick and the Cavendish family, later the Dukes of Newcastle. The great halls at Wollaton and Worksop were built in the 1580s, the former with money made from the Willoughby family's coal mines. Thoresby was bought in 1633, but Clumber was not established until the 18th century.

Charles I

The latter stages of Charles I's reign saw him at loggerheads with Parliament over matters of finance, religion and the rights of the individual. His main support was in the north, and he needed to raise an army to march against Parliament. The nearest he could safely get to London at the outset was Nottingham, and consequently on 22 August 1642 he unfurled his banner on Standard Hill, above the castle. He had solid support from the Notts gentry, but many smaller families were for Cromwell. The Hutchinsons and Iretons of Attenborough helped to man the Roundheads' garrison at Nottingham Castle, while the Royalists had control of Newark. Thus, each side controlled one crossing of the River Trent. Although no major battles were fought on Nottinghamshire soil, Newark was the site of a large siege that only ended when the King surrendered after spending his last night at the Saracen's Head in Southwell. Surprisingly there was little change to the county afterwards, and only small amounts of land changed hands. The restoration of Charles II completed the return to normality and the dominance of the landowners

Smelting

The Civil war had damaged large tracts of the forest, and the coming of large scale iron smelting saw the destruction of many trees for charcoal.

In Birklands, 50,000 oaks in 1609 were reduced to 37,000 by 1686, and 10,000 by 1780. Coal mining saw small villages turned into towns, and Nottingham's population was rising rapidly.

Meanwhile the Dukeries were well established, with Clumber Park enclosed in 1707. Towards the end of the 18th century the Chesterfield and Erewash canals were built and the Nottingham and Grantham canals started, enabling the easy transportation of coal and other cargoes. It was also about this time when the enclosure act saw hedgerows appear to divide up the great open fields and commons. Framework knitting and lace manufacturing grew in importance as a cottage industry in the south, but the poor wages and conditions fermented the riots that were a feature of the 1780s and 1790s.

The Lace Centre, Severns Building (Courtesy of Nottingham City Council)

The great mills were built and, at Papplewick, Watt's steam engine of 1785 remains as a great tourist attraction to this day. It was the first such engine of its kind in the country. John Leavers' invention of the automatic lace machine revolutionised the industry, and there are excellent examples of it the Wollaton Park Industrial Museum.

Nottingham Castle

Nottingham Castle had, by now, been replaced by a rather grand Palace. But the petition by its owner, the Duke of Newcastle, against the Reform Bill which was to have introduced political representation to the common man, resulted in an angry mob's burning it down. The blackened ruin was left to rot for many years to shame the townspeople, before being restored to its present state.

The county has much to offer the tourist. There are excellent museums in Nottingham, the parks of Clumber, Thoresby, Newstead and Wollaton. The small market centres of Bingham, Newark, Retford, Southwell, and Worksop are ideal setting-off points for the countryside. Sherwood Forest and Robin Hood are as appealing as ever to the visitor and The Robin Hood Way (see below) makes for very pleasant walking. There are dozens of literary connections associated with the county, but the two best-known are Lord Byron and D.H. Lawrence. Their lives and works are chronicled elsewhere, but it is interesting that both would have walked some of the areas chosen by the authors of this book.

Changing Pattern

Nottinghamshire has a changing pattern of industry. The coal industry is in a state of severe decline, and the effect on the many pit villages could be very marked. But the leisure industry is thriving, and local companies such as Boots have become household names throughout the land. It is becoming increasingly important as a business centre with firms leaving the south to set up here.

Nottingham is one of the top three cities in England, according to the polls, and thoroughly deserves its reputation as the Queen of the East Midlands. It makes an ideal destination for a short break and offers a good base for those choosing to explore the surrounding countryside.

The Council House and Square (Courtesy of Nottingham City Council)

Longer Walks

Nottinghamshire has two long-distance footpaths, the Robin Hood Way and the Trent Valley Way. The former is 88 miles long, from Nottingham Castle to Edwinstowe, by a circuitous route. It takes in most of the major features of the county and the reader will meet its distinctive green waymarks on several of our walks mentioned in this book. Most of the route can be tackled in easy stretches using public transport and there is an excellent guidebook available. Beware, though, that it only lists the pubs of the sponsoring brewery, which are not always the best in the vicinity.

The Trent Valley Way hugs the river closely where possible, although in places the walker will meet the blue waymarkers with the Trent nowhere to be seen. It runs for 84 miles, from Long Eaton to West

Stockwith. In addition, there are many waymarked paths, Yellow Arrows for footpaths and Blue Arrows for bridlepaths. Leaflets and books, some of them free, can be obtained at libraries and the Tourist Offices.

However, the best way to walk, apart from this book of course, is simply to use the O.S. maps and make up your own routes.

Pub Walks

The walks in this book vary in length from 3 to 11 miles and for the most part are easy going. They usually begin at and pass through rural villages and this is one of the many pluses about walking in Nottinghamshire. The villages are steeped in history. There are thirty rambles to choose from and most are circular.

Wherever possible, we have attempted to avoid duplication with other publications such as the superb set of walks leaflets published by the County Council or books such as "Newark and Sherwood Rambles" by Malcome Mckenzie (Sigma Leisure) which includes 30 well-researched walks in the Newark area. The County Council (Leisure Services) have a programme of guided walks for those not used to walking to join others on a series of walks in different parts of the county.

Details are available from local tourist information offices.

Let us not forget the work of The Ramblers Association in encouraging everyone- landowners, parish and county councils to maintain a network of paths open for our enjoyment. Those wishing to find out more about the Ramblers should write contact them at 1/5 Wandsworth Road, London, SW8 2XX or telephone 071 582 6878

There are a few golden rules to remember. Do not trust the weather. Always go prepared with a waterproof and warm clothing. It is easy enough to take a light rucksack with the waterproofs and a light snack in case the walk takes longer than you first imagined.

The walks should be easy to follow by simply using a good map and the instructions in the book. There are two main problems regarding instructions for the reader. The first relates to how the authors perceive the route and describe it. They might consider a green lane to be the main feature and write this up accordingly. But, you might think that some tractor tracks were the way ahead and therefore miss the intended route. If you do find yourself off the prescribed route, retrace your steps to a point where you found the text to be absolutely clear and then look again at the points mentioned by the authors to aid navigation. We quite expect you to curse us more than once!

The second point relates to when things change. As the countryside is a working environment, field patterns, areas of woodland and buildings change. Please accept our apologies in advance for this. The text has been written so that even if a hedge is grubbed up or a woodland felled, the way should still be easy to follow, despite the loss of an occasional landmark.

The Pubs

One of the great joys of any walk is to adjourn to a local hostelry for a tasty pint of beer (or other beverage) either at the end of the day or as a respite during the afternoon. Inns have, for centuries, welcomed the traveller on foot: tradespeople, farmers, miners and quarrymen going to or from their daily work. Now, the country pub is geared to leisure, although many still look after a local working population.

Despite a shift in customer base, the tradition of hospitality and keeping of good beer remains. Here, we owe a good deal to The Campaign For Real Ale (CAMRA), which has for the past 22 years has championed the cause of the real ale drinker and the retention of characterful local pubs. This organisation has done more for the discerning drinker than most big breweries would care to admit. Those wishing to join should contact CAMRA at 34 Alma Road, St Albans, Herts, AL1 3BW, Telephone (0727) 867201.

Tipple

There is a one little problem, of course, for the rambler who loves real ale. Beer and driving do not mix. All of the rambles in this book feature a pub and several mention two or more along the way. Those readers who find it impossible to pass a pub without sampling a tipple, should let someone else do the driving. Better still, do as the authors did when researching this volume- use the local bus or train. Some parts of Nottinghamshire enjoy a better service now than in the late 1970s when some of the authors were researching material for a little booklet "Beer, Boots and Buses".

The use of local buses and trains does help to keep congestion down, conserve energy and minimise pollution and puts money into a vital local facility. The authors endorse wholeheartedly the Countrygoer concept, a campaign to encourage countryside lovers to leave their car at home whenever there is a bus or train alternative. This can add to the fun of the day and many of the walks included are accessible by public transport every day of the week – Sundays too!

Here is the main contact number should you require up-to-the-minute information: (0602) 240000

All of the pubs mentioned in full in each chapter of this book have been approached by the authors to ensure that details of opening times and the like are accurate at the time of writing.

Most country pubs in the land have changed in the past two to three decades to survive. The first major change is that most pubs serve food and this has become so important to their trading pattern that publicans do not allow people, ramblers or otherwise, to eat food bought on their premises. Most of the pubs in this book offer bar meals at lunch and in the evening but not usually the entire session, more likely noon until 2pm and from 7pm until 9pm to 9.30pm. Unless stated in the text the pub concerned does not allow eating your own (food that is) on the premises.

The same applies to muddy boots. Some walkers now use trainers or similar footwear particularly in summer. In the winter, boots and wellies are more common; these might be all right in the public bar but lounges and open plan rooms tend to be carpeted. Thus, it makes sense to take off your boots before entering to avoid the offence of being asked to do this.

The question of families in pubs often arises. Every publican in the book is happy to welcome families, especially if children are well behaved. Most have gardens or outdoor seats for summer use and this is ideal for the family group. Children are also welcome indoors if there is a separate area or room away from the bar. This is currently the law. Children under the age of 14 are not allowed in bars. Thus, it makes sense for mum or dad to simply pop a head around the door to ask whether it is all right bring the family in! Some hostelries feel they are not always geared up and say so. We list the details in the text.

However you decide to travel, and wherever you decide to imbibe the authors hope that you have as much fun walking these routes as they had when researching them.

Enjoy the Walks!

1. SUTTON BONINGTON

Route: Sutton Bonington – River Soar – Zouch – Sutton Bonington

Distance: 4.5 miles

Map: O.S. Pathfinder 853 (Loughborough, North, and Castle Donington)

Start: St. Michael's Church, Main Street (Grid Reference: SK504254)

Access: Sutton Bonington lies 11 miles South West of Nottingham; 3 miles South East of Junction 24 on the M1. On arrival in Sutton Bonington by car it is possible to park on Main Street or in a small car park signposted "Bottle Bank and Playing Field" off Main Street.

Bus Services from Nottingham and Loughborough run hourly throughout the day to Sutton Bonington. For travel information, contact Barton Coaches on 0602 240000.

The Anchor Inn, Bollards Lane, Sutton Bonington (0509 673648)

This is an attractive pub serving excellent Marstons ales, in a side lane off Main Street. There is a pleasant garden area overlooking the church, and children are welcome in the garden, although there is no family room available. Bar snacks are available during lunchtime openings. The Anchor is open at lunchtimes between Monday and Friday inclusive from noon until 3 pm. It opens at 7pm in the evening. There is all-day Saturday opening from mid-day and the usual Sunday hours apply. This is an inn of some character – the pub is reputedly haunted where good ale can be supped in relaxing surroundings.

The Rose and Crown, Zouch (0509 842240)

This pub, set on the side of the canal at Zouch, has an attractive outdoor area overlooking the canal, and welcomes families both inside and outside. The Rose and Crown serves meals throughout the lunchtime and evening opening hours; lunchtime specials are available. The real ales available are Theakstons XB, Youngers No.3 and Home Ale Bitter; the latter was particularly fine at the time of visit. The Rose and Crown is open from 11.30 a.m. until 3pm and from 6.30pm on Mondays to Saturdays. Usual Sunday hours are observed.

The Rose and Crown

Sutton Bonington

Sutton Bonington is a South Nottinghamshire rural community close to the River Soar and the Leicestershire border. The Church of St. Michael's is particularly attractive, and can be viewed from the beer garden of the Anchor Inn (see above). Both Main Street and Soar Lane contain many fine old buildings; indeed, 1 Soar Lane bears the date 1661. This is a timber frame house with long first floor windows, inserted to light a framework knitting workshop. It is believed that Matthias Simpkin, a successful wool merchant from Norwich, and his descendants occupied this house between 1696 and 1805. From this house the family supplied outworkers in all the surrounding villages with the necessary articles for their trade. There is a very good local booklet available "Discover Sutton Bonnington – Past and Present" by the local historical society.

Zouch

The hamlet of Zouch is an example of a small canal settlement. You can see, to the right of the Rose and Crown, the wharf which was used for loading and unloading goods of the canal trade. Most of the village of Zouch lies within Leicestershire beyond the Zouch bridge, which marks the county boundary. The Rose and Crown lies, however, in Nottinghamshire. Records of a bridge at this point go back to the 13th Century. The present bridge was opened in 1931.

The Walk

(1) The walk commences from St Michael's church on Main Street, a few yards from the bus stop, stand with your back to the church and then turn right up Main Street. Temptation lurks in Bollards Lane in the shape of the Anchor Inn.

(2) However, the walk continues up Main Street, and then left down Soar Lane to the left of a public telephone box (see below for an alternative). Follow the Lane until a bridge is crossed, the footpath is then immediately on your left. Take a stick with you on the path over the fields, as the way may be overgrown with nettles towards the end. The path bears diagonally across a field towards a stile.

On crossing this, you can see your way across the next field to another stile. Once over this stile the path lies towards the right of the field and under a set of power lines and a stile. Go over the stile and walk directly ahead towards a pylon and a white house in the distance. Again a stile awaits but this time incorporating a wooden bridge. Once across this, the path follows the hedge on the left of the field (this field contains crops but the path is easily located). The path continues alongside the hedge across an overgrown area, towards a stile and bridge accessing the River Soar.

** Alternatively, to enjoy a gentler walk, follow Soar Lane for one mile all the way to the River Soar. Turn left along the river bank past the marina, picking up the route again opposite the white pub buildings on the opposite bank.

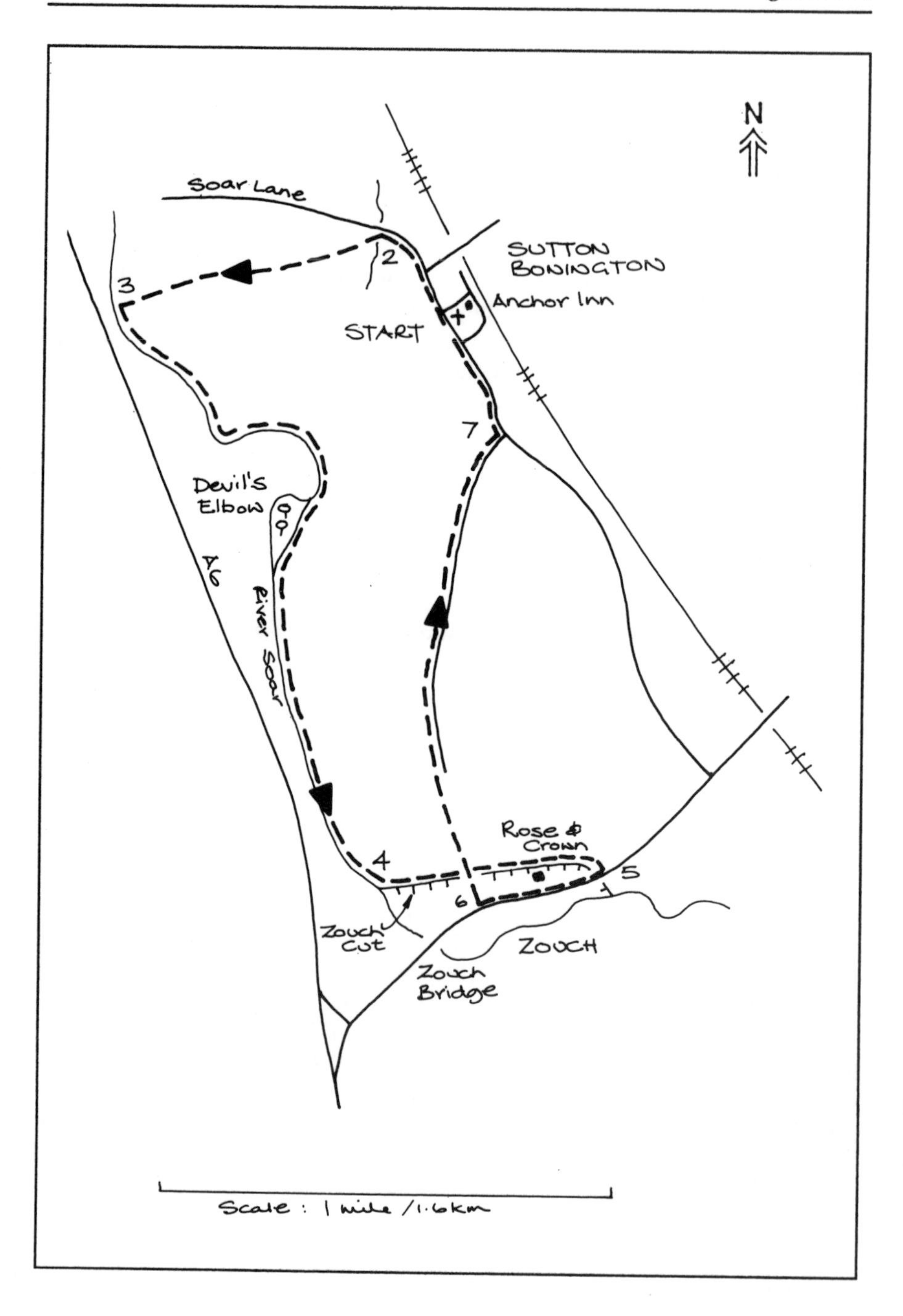
N
Soar Lane
SUTTON
BONINGTON
Anchor Inn
START
2
3
7
Devil's
Elbow
A6
River Soar
Rose & Crown
4
5
6
Zouch Cut
ZOUCH
Zouch Bridge
Scale : 1 mile / 1.6km

(3) Once on the river bank turn left along the towpath. Walk on past the "Devils Elbow" where water surrounds an island. There are many stiles to be crossed while walking through the fields that edge the river. After about a mile and half, you will reach a point where the "Zouch Cut" leaves the river to provide a navigation for boats avoiding the weirs on the river; we also leave the river at this point to follow the Cut. Pass over a stile and follow the towpath past the lock.

(4) On your right you will see the Zouch bridge, and further to the right on the River Soar, a boat club. Continue along the towpath, passing under the bridge that carries a bridleway. On the opposite bank you will see the Rose and Crown public house, which can be your next port of call.

(5) At the bridge leave the towpath and turn right towards the Rose and Crown. On leaving the Rose and Crown turn right and continue along the main road to Zouch for 400 metres. Most of the village of Zouch lies beyond the Zouch bridge and is in Leicestershire, but the Rose and Crown and surroundings lie within Nottinghamshire. You will see a bridleway signposted to the right, leading over a field towards the Zouch cut.

(6) Take this bridleway and pass up and over the Zouch cut on the footbridge. Continue straight ahead along the bridleway. After 400 metres the bridleway opens out; continue straight ahead and pass through the gateway. This bridleway eventually becomes a minor road, and leads you into Pasture Lane back in Sutton Bonington.

(7) The grocery store on your left used to be a smithy, one of three in the village. On the right stands a whitebeam tree which was planted to commemorate the Silver Jubilee of George the Fifth in 1935. You can rest underneath it on the thoughtfully provided benches. Turn left into Main Street, and immediately on your left lies the Kings Head public house. This has an outdoor garden and drinking area, in addition to very interesting maps on the lounge bar wall. A short walk further along Main Street returns you to the car park by the playing fields and St. Michael's Church.

2. WEST LEAKE

Route: West Leake – West Leake Hills – West Leake

Distance: 4.5 miles (woodland and farmland)

Map: O.S. Pathfinder 853 (Loughborough (North) and Castle Donington)

Start: Star Public House, West Leake (Grid Reference: SK 523261)

Access: West Leake is 10 miles South West of Nottingham; 5 miles North of Loughborough.

West Leake is served by a bus service from Nottingham and Loughborough.

There is a car park at the Star public house, but this is for patrons only. Alternative car parking is available on the road in the village of West Leake itself.

The Star, West Leake – also known locally as 'The Pit House' (0509 852233)

The Star is a very attractive 250 year old pub with two bars of great character, displaying much beautiful old wood. Food is served at lunchtimes (Monday to Friday only), and children are welcome inside if eating. Otherwise there are plenty of benches in front of the pub, and other tables in a grassed patio area on the other side of the car park. The Star is known locally as The Pit House. Excellent draught Bass is sold, and Adnams Bitter is available for the thirsty rambler. The Star is open from noon until 2.30pm daily and from 6pm in the evenings except on Sundays, when the evening opening is at 7pm.

West Leake

West Leake is a very attractive village settlement, which rates mention in the Domesday Book as Leche: the name of the stream that flows through the village. There is a pleasant church that was restored in 1878 and has elements dating from the 12th Century. West Leake has been allowed to retain its gentle rural character, while its younger and brasher sibling, East Leake, has developed into a small town.

The Star

The Walk

(1) The walk begins at The Star Public House. From the Star bear left down the road signposted to West Leake village, and walk through the village along the main street.

(2) At the end of the main street the road bears sharply to the right, and a bridleway leads straight ahead. There is limited parking space here, but ensure that you do not obstruct agricultural vehicles. Take the bridleway, and ignore another bridleway signposted to the left after 50 yards. Follow the bridleway upwards, with the West Leake hills to be seen up ahead. Continue following the bridleway, keeping to the left of the hedge.

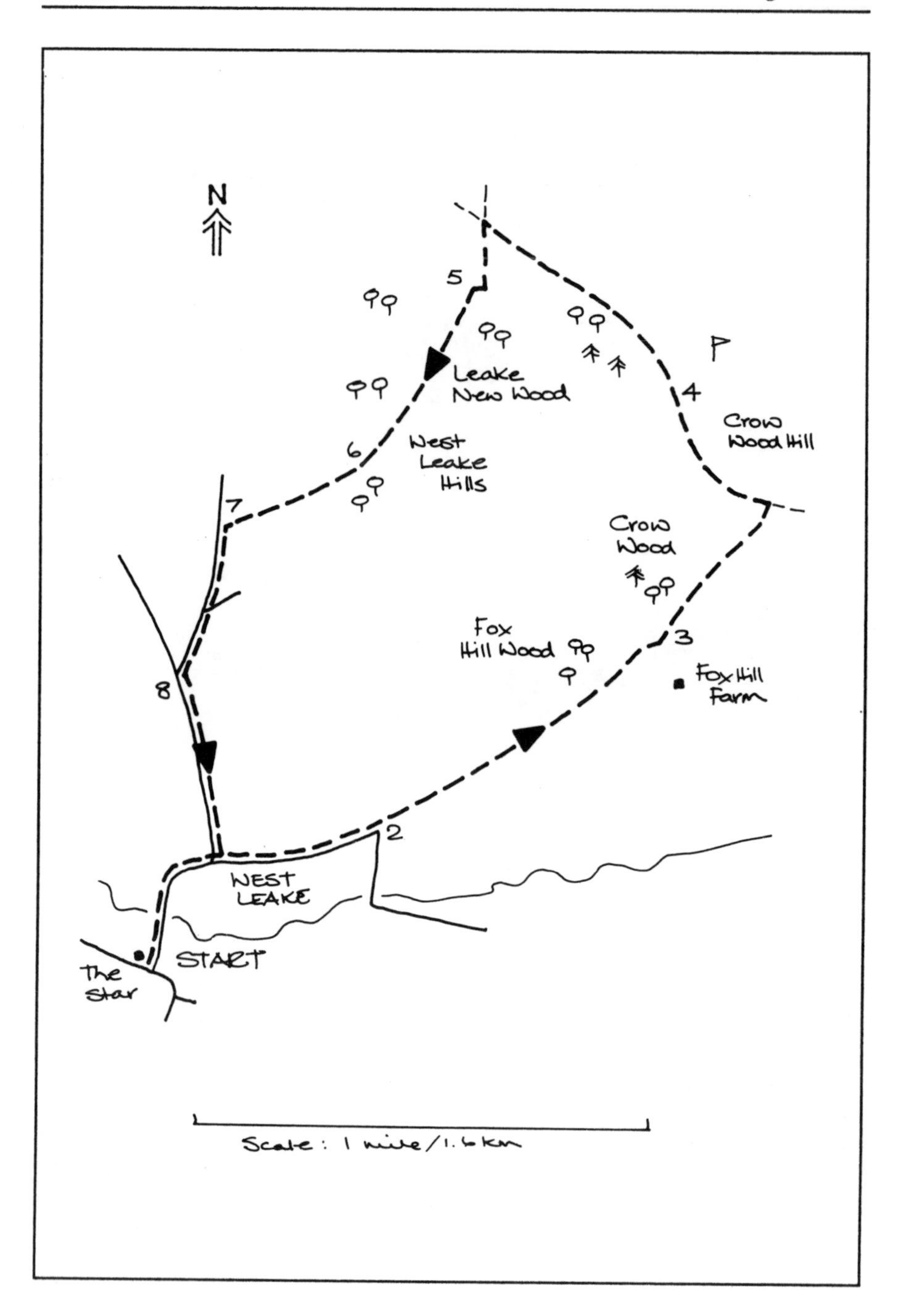
N
5
Leake
New Wood
4
Crow
Wood Hill
6
West
Leake
Hills
7
Crow
Wood
Fox
Hill Wood
3
Fox Hill
Farm
8
2
WEST
LEAKE
START
The
Star
Scale: 1 mile/1.6 km

(3) Fox Hill Farm now becomes visible to the right; Fox Hill Wood is to the left. When level with Fox Hill Farm, turn left along the stoned bridleway. Continue along the bridleway, ignoring the path leading off to the left behind Crow Wood. At the end of the bridleway at the junction, turn left and continue walking. Views are visible towards Gotham on the right. This is the top of Crow Wood Hill. Note the golf course on the right enjoying fine views over the Nottinghamshire countryside, before your path turns bosky for a while.

(4) The path emerges from the wood and runs to the left of the golf course. Walk to the left of the tee of the fourth hole. There are views to the right towards the City of Nottingham, famed for lace and bicycles. Continue to the left of the red brick building on the golf course. Walk to the left of the 4th green; this is a long and difficult hole! Follow the footpath sign, as the path leads through young woodland. Pass through the gate (it may be muddy here). Keep the hedge to your left. At the end of the field turn left through the gate, and then walk straight ahead keeping the hedge to your right. Ignore the path, the blue marker and the gate to your right after passing through this gate.

(5) Pass through the gate at the end of the field and turn right. Twenty-five metres further on, turn left and follow the path down through Leake New Wood and West Leake Hills. Ignore all paths off to either side and continue straight along this broad bridleway. The path dips steeply downhill.

(6) At the bottom of the hill continue straight ahead, crossing over a track. Keep to the left-hand edge of the field along a well delineated track with a hedge and ditch immediately to the left. At the end of the field, go straight on through a gap in the hedge; again keeping the hedge on your left and go past a clump of three trees. Ratcliffe on Soar power station can be seen in the distance to your right.

(7) At the end of the field, cross a rickety footbridge onto a gravelled bridleway, and turn left along it. After a couple of hundred yards when the path splits, take the right-hand fork.

(8) Where the bridleway meets the main road, turn left along it for half a mile until you reach a junction. Turn left and walk through the village if you parked your car there. If not, turn right and follow the road for 300 metres, ignoring the turning to the right, and following the bend to the left to reach The Star and the bus stop.

3. WYSALL

Route: Wysall – Thorpe-in-the-Glebe – Wysall

Distance: 3 miles

Map: O.S. Pathfinder 854 (Scalford and Nether Broughton)

Start: The Plough, Wysall (Grid Reference: SK 604273)

Access: Wysall is situated 11 miles South East of Nottingham. There is parking for patrons only in the large car park opposite The Plough Inn at the North end of the village. There is limited parking space available on the Main Street by the telephone box and before the village hall.

Wysall is connected to Nottingham by a regular hourly bus service. (0602 240000).

The Plough, Wysall (0509 880339)

This is a beautiful country pub, renowned for its hanging baskets and barrows of flowers. Food is served every lunchtime, although rolls only are available on Sundays. Families are welcomed and there is an attractive beer garden. A wide range of real ales is available: Draught Bass, Marstons Pedigree, Vaux Samson Ale and Stones Cask Bitter. The Plough is open from 11 a.m. until 3.30pm on Mondays to Saturdays and from 6pm in the evenings. Usual Sunday hours. This really is a delightful spot on a Summer's evening

Wysall

Wysall is one of the three "Thankful Villages" in Nottinghamshire: of the 17 local men who went to serve in the First World War, all returned safely. The clock on the church tower commemorates this happy outcome. Wysall has no formal roll of honour on display in the village, but each man who answered his country's call in the Great War was presented with a silver inkstand. On this was engraved his name and the words "with gratitude from Wysall for answering Duty's call in the Great War".

Wysall is an attractive country village mentioned in the Domesday Book as *Wysoc*. Its population has relied on agricultural activities throughout the ages but commuting has increased in recent years.

The church, Wysall

The Walk

(1) Walk South along the Main Road away from The Plough. Pass Wysall and Thorpe Village Hall on your left. Turn left at the road junction signposted to Wymeswold opposite the church.

Continue along the road, taking care when walking along the roadway after the pavement peters out. Walk past the name sign of Thorpe in the Glebe; an ancient parish.

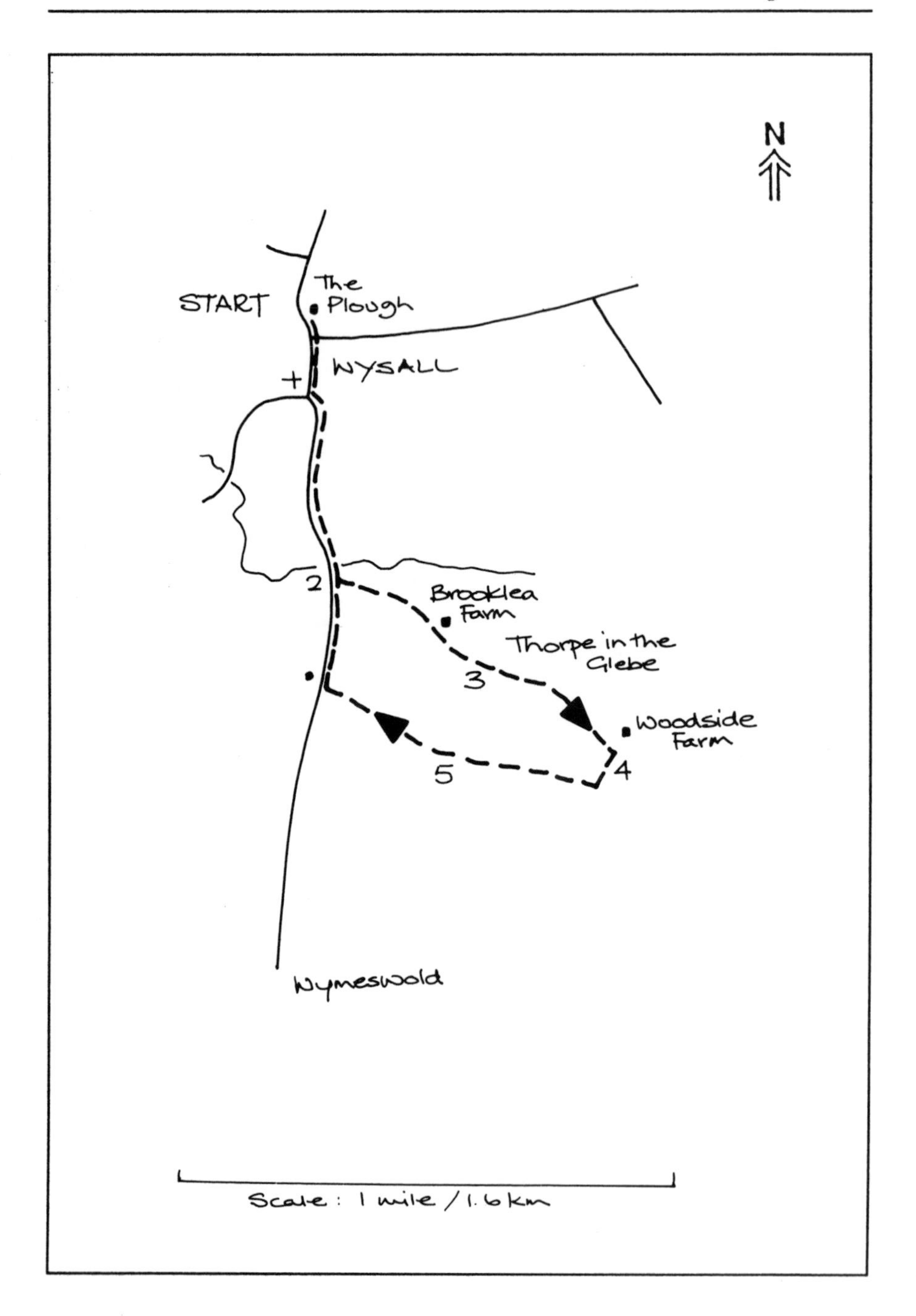
N
START
The Plough
WYSALL
2
Brooklea Farm
Thorpe in the Glebe
3
Woodside Farm
4
5
Wymeswold
Scale : 1 mile / 1.6km

(2) Turn left down the track immediately on your left with a sign on the gate reading Crooklea Farm. The track bears to the right through a caravan park. A stile and a public footpath lie to your right; bear left over the field towards a waymarked post just to the left of a tree. The path crosses the next field rightwards towards the corner. Pass over the stile to your right – do not climb over the new fencing directly in the corner of the field!

(3) Keep to the left-hand edge of the field and walk towards a stile. Keep to the left of the field; pass over a wooden footbridge, and follow the path that bears rightwards over the field. (The path cuts diagonally over the field, but local people traditionally walk around the edge of the field). Pass through the gate at the corner of the field and continue straight on keeping to the right-hand edge of the field. Just before the end of the field, pass over a stile to your right through the hedge. Make your way diagonally across this field, following the line of the telegraph poles, towards the stile at the gap in the hedge. Cut straight across the corner of the field to the next stile. Pass over this, and walk a further fifty metres ahead to the next stile. (This stile may be obscured by goats, a caravan, and other pieces of farm equipment).

(4) Pass over this stile and turn immediately right, hugging the right-hand field margin as far as the corner of the field. At the corner of the field turn right immediately before the gate, ignoring the waymarked path straight on. Cross over two fields keeping to the left-hand field margin with the hedge directly to your left. Pass over a wooden stile into a grassy lane and continue straight ahead. Pass by the Frank Hind Field Centre hut to your left, and pass through a metal gate.

(5) Turn directly right and walk along the right-hand edge of the field, keeping the hedge directly to your right. Ignore the footpath that leads off over a stile to your right. Continue through a succession of fields, always keeping to the right-hand edge, until you reach the Wysall – Wymeswold main road. Turn right along here, and retrace your steps towards the village of Wysall, and a well-earned refreshment in The Plough.

4. GOTHAM

Route: Gotham – Thrumpton – Barton in Fabis – Gotham

Distance: 6 miles (woodland and farmland)

Map: O.S. Pathfinder 833 (Nottingham (South West))

Start: Cuckoo Bush Inn, Gotham (Grid Reference: SK536302)

Access: Gotham is 5 miles south-west of Nottingham. Car parking is available on the small square opposite the Cuckoo Bush Inn, and opposite the Sun Inn.

Gotham is connected to Nottingham and Loughborough by a regular bus service. Phone 0602 503665 for travel details.

The Cuckoo Bush, Gotham (0602 830306)

The Cuckoo Bush Inn is a very attractive village inn, serving a very enjoyable pint of Bass. There are many tales attaching to the pub and the village of Gotham itself. The pub sign shows the villagers of Gotham building a hedge around a cuckoo, so that it would stay and sing to them. The Cuckoo Bush serves food every lunchtime, and welcomes families. There is an outdoor area/garden. Opening hours are 12.00 noon to 3.00pm and 6.00pm to 11.00pm Monday to Saturday, with normal Sunday opening. The landlord is also willing to open at other permitted times upon request.

Gotham

Many strange activities are laid at the door of Gotham people, who were said to have deliberately behaved like idiots to avoid the attentions of King John and his tax inspectors. Strangely enough, both the major contenders in the 1992 American Presidential elections, Bill Clinton and George Bush, were found to have ancestors in Gotham. The church and well on the small village square form a particularly fine focal point.

The Walk

(1) The walk starts outside the Cuckoo Bush Inn in Gotham. When facing the Cuckoo Bush, turn to the right and start to walk along the main road to Nottingham.

(2) Turn left after about 100 metres at junction signed for Kingston, Kegworth Road. There is a South Nottingham bus stop here if arriving by public transport. About 200 metres down this road is an old school building on the right, the footpath is immediately before this and is signed. Turn right onto the footpath, through a gate labelled School House Drive. The path takes you past the School House, now a private dwelling, and over a stile down into a cutting. The path crosses this cutting, taking you behind a bench and up out of the cutting slightly to the right. Follow the path along the right-hand edge of a field. Gotham village is now laid out behind you.

(3) At the end of the field there are steps up to a stile, once over the stile, the path is diagonally left up the hill. Continue up the hill keeping the trees of Round Spinney to your right. At this point you are at an altitude in excess of 90 metres – highly elevated for Nottinghamshire. Over a stile bear left across the field towards the trees. Cross over the stile into Gotham Hill Woods; the path goes diagonally left from the stile. The woods are beautifully green in summer with light filtering though the trees, providing a contrast to the previous open landscape. On reaching a fork in the path, take the right-hand downward sloping path. There is a footpath marker at this point. The path now descends steeply through the wood, and can be slippery in wet weather conditions. The path then veers to the left and becomes altogether gentler in its descent. You emerge from the wood into a field; cross over a stile to the right and follow along the left-hand edge of the field; the River Trent may be viewed in the distance ahead. At the end of the field bear left along path and then turn right to take a footbridge over the A523.

(4) Once across the bridge turn left onto a minor road then, at a junction with a white-painted house on the left and signposted Thrumpton, turn right. An attractive lane leads through the village, past the village hall and bearing right round the church. The road passes the entrance to Thrumpton Hall, which was owned for centuries by the Powtrell family.

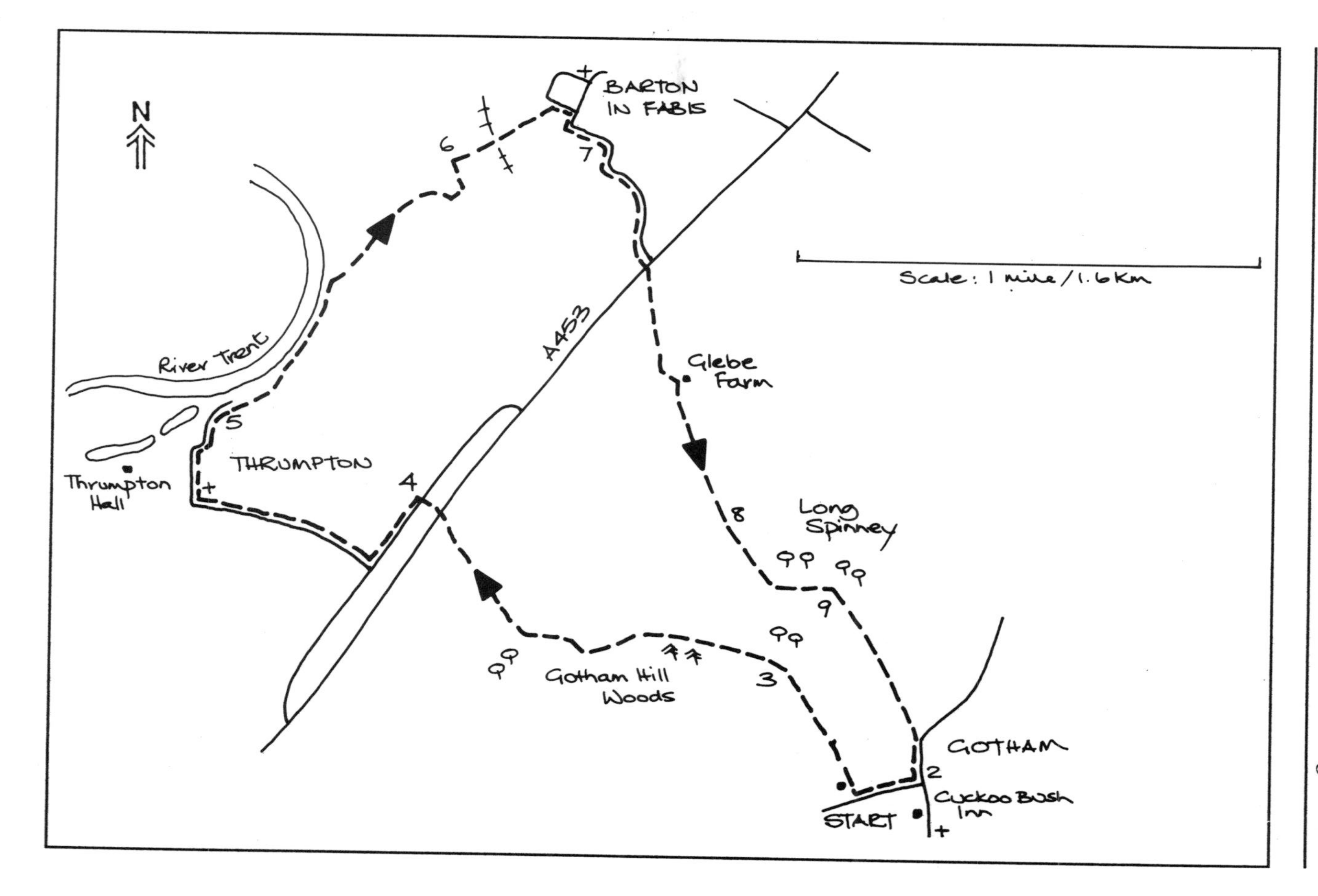
N
BARTON IN FABIS
6
7
Scale: 1 mile/1.6 Km
River Trent
A453
Glebe Farm
5
THRUMPTON
Thrumpton Hall
4
8
Long Spinney
9
Gotham Hill Woods
3
GOTHAM
2
Cuckoo Bush Inn
START

They lost all their estates, however, because of their involvement in the Gunpowder Plot. The road continues past a high flood marker.

(5) Pass over a stile joining the Trent Valley Way, and deviate from the roadway to walk along the wide grassy banks of the Trent, observing the ducks and fishermen, who often brave the waters of the Trent complete with waders. On reaching a left-hand bend in the river, complete with navigation markers for boats, there is a fence; turn right here, away from the river bank. There is a gate in the fence and next to it a stile; cross the stile and turn right along the side of the field. After the next stile, walk along a narrow footpath between the fields with a hedge to the right. Pass through a gate, and the path carries on to the right around the field margin. The path takes you through two left turns around the edge of the field before you turn right to resume the direction of travel.

(6) The path then bears right over a bridge across a drainage ditch, before bearing diagonally across a field towards Barton in Fabis, crossing the possible route of an old railway line. Two stiles lead into a farmyard; pass through this farmyard and cross a stile onto the road where you turn right. At the junction turn right to continue the walk (if you turn left the village of Barton in Fabis is reached – however there is NO pub).

The Barton Ferry crossing may have been in use since Roman times, as many remains have been discovered in this area. It is believed that Charles the First, fleeing to Scotland in 1646, crossed the River Trent here in his anxiety to avoid the City of Nottingham and the risk of detection and capture.

(7) Once you have turned right follow the road that bears left and through fields towards the main A523 road. With care, cross over the main road, and the footpath continues along a farm track on the other side. This track leads you through Glebe Farm and climbs slightly uphill. The remains of a Roman pavement were once uncovered at Glebe Farm. The track then passes through a pig farm – don't be startled by the odd snort from the pigs. Continue along the track uphill and straight ahead past the farm buildings.

(8) About fifty yards past the last shed, cross a stile to your left; the path bears upwards diagonally across the field towards a telegraph pole. At the top of the field a stile is located to the left of the trees and hedge,

cross this stile. From this position, there are superb views back over the Trent valley. Once over this stile, bear right, straight ahead over the field until you reach another stile. Cross this and follow a path alongside the trees of Long Spinney. This path bears left with the wood. You then take a path down the hill, diagonally rightwards across the field towards a metal gate.

(9) Pass through this gate and turn right onto track. Follow this track for about a quarter of a mile until it ends back in the village of Gotham. The Windmill pub is to your left. Follow main road straight ahead towards the church; the Sun Inn lies on the square to left, serving a fine range of Everard ales, whilst the Cuckoo Bush lies to the right.

The Gatehouse, Barton in Fabis

5. KINOULTON

Route: Kinoulton – Grantham Canal – Wild's Bridge – Spencer's Bridge – Owthorpe Road – Colston Bassett – Hall Farm – Kinoulton

Distance: 6 miles

Map: O.S. Pathfinder 834 (Radcliffe on Trent & Keyworth)

Start: The Nevile Arms, Kinoulton (Grid Reference SK 682311)

Access: Kinoulton is signposted off the A46 via Owthorpe. There is limited on street parking in the village but please park considerately. There is a Barton's bus service on the Market Drayton road at Widmerpool, adding a further mile on to the route in each direction.

The Nevile Arms, Kinoulton (0949 81236)

The Nevile Arms stands at a junction under the shade of a large oak, a large Hardys and Hansons pub that retains a lounge and bar, the latter geared up for those who enjoy pub games. Its name reflects the importance of the landowning Nevile family, the Earls of Gainsborough, who were major benefactors towards the building of the present church. In the late 1920s the pub was bought by Jesse Hind. Relishing his latest possession he renamed it The Hind Arms, much to the annoyance of the regulars who petitioned for its old name back. As we see, they won, and the coat of arms of the Gainsboroughs can still be seen. All of this history is thirsty work so you will find Kimberley Classic is on handpull at the bar. Food is served from Tuesdays to Saturdays between 11.45am and 2pm and from 6pm until 9pm in the evenings. Families are welcome and there is a very pleasant and sheltered garden to the rear of the pub. Opening times are from 11am until 3pm at lunch and from 6pm in the evening on weekdays. Usual Sunday opening hours.

The Martins Arms Inn, Colston Bassett (0949 81361)

This delightfully situated inn has been featured in many editions of the Good Beer Guide, an inn renowned for its quality food as much as its well kept beer. To the left of the main entrance is a restaurant and to the right a carpeted lounge where there is fine woodwork including the magnificent wooden fire surround that gives the room a very distinctive character. In Summer a door opens out from this room to a large sheltered garden where visitors can sit back and watch the world go by. The range of draught beers on offer is wide: Marstons Best Bitter, Border Bitter and Pedigree, Batemans XB and XXXB, and Bass. Bar food and the restaurant are available from noon until 2pm daily and from 6.30 until 10pm each night except Sunday. Families are welcome but not in the bar. The hosts say that there is a well respected ghost on the top floor, a lady in grey but they have not seen her yet personally! The Martins Arms Inn is open from noon until 3pm on Mondays to Saturdays, and from 6pm in the evening. Usual Sunday hours prevail.

Kinoulton

This linear village lining the road from the Fosse Way to the village green complete with seat and spreading oak has not altered much over the decades. The proposal for a golf course on the outskirts might change things but otherwise this sleepy settlement is home mainly to people who work in nearby towns. The original church was set in the hillside a respectable walk away from the village but this fell into ruin and a red brick church was built in Georgian times to replace it. One yarn suggests that the villagers used some materials of the old church in their own re-building programmes. This included the baker who is said to have lined his oven with headstones, a matter that was raised when one of his customers noted the phrase "In loving memory " imprinted on her loaf. It never caught on!

Colston Bassett

One of the great landowning families of the area, the Bassetts have given rise to the village name and Colston Bassett Hall stands in sweeping parkland near the village. Here stands the ruined church of St Mary that fell into disrepair during the eighteenth century. A century later when times had improved, the new church, St John the Divine, was built; a handsome church funded by the then owner of the hall, Robert Knowles, the High Sheriff of Nottinghamshire. He built the church partly to commemorate the untimely death of his eldest son John at 21 in a drowning accident. Colston Bassett is known for the traditional production of farmhouse Stilton; this is on sale at the village post office which looks out to the old village cross, medieval in origin but restored in 1831.

The Cross, Colston Bassett

The Walk

(1) From the Nevile Arms turn right to walk along the road to the Grantham Canal, passing the church on the right. Follow the towpath on the right of the canal although there is a footpath on the left bank too. The canal reaches the bridge allowing access to Vimy Ridge farm on the left. On the right is a dusty lane lined with gently swaying poplars, a scene meant to be reminiscent of the battlefield of Flanders. Jesse Hind, the same man who bought the Nevile Arms mentioned above, planted these in memory of the death of one of his sons at the Somme in 1916. It is said that 188 trees were planted in all, reflecting the number of officers killed in action.

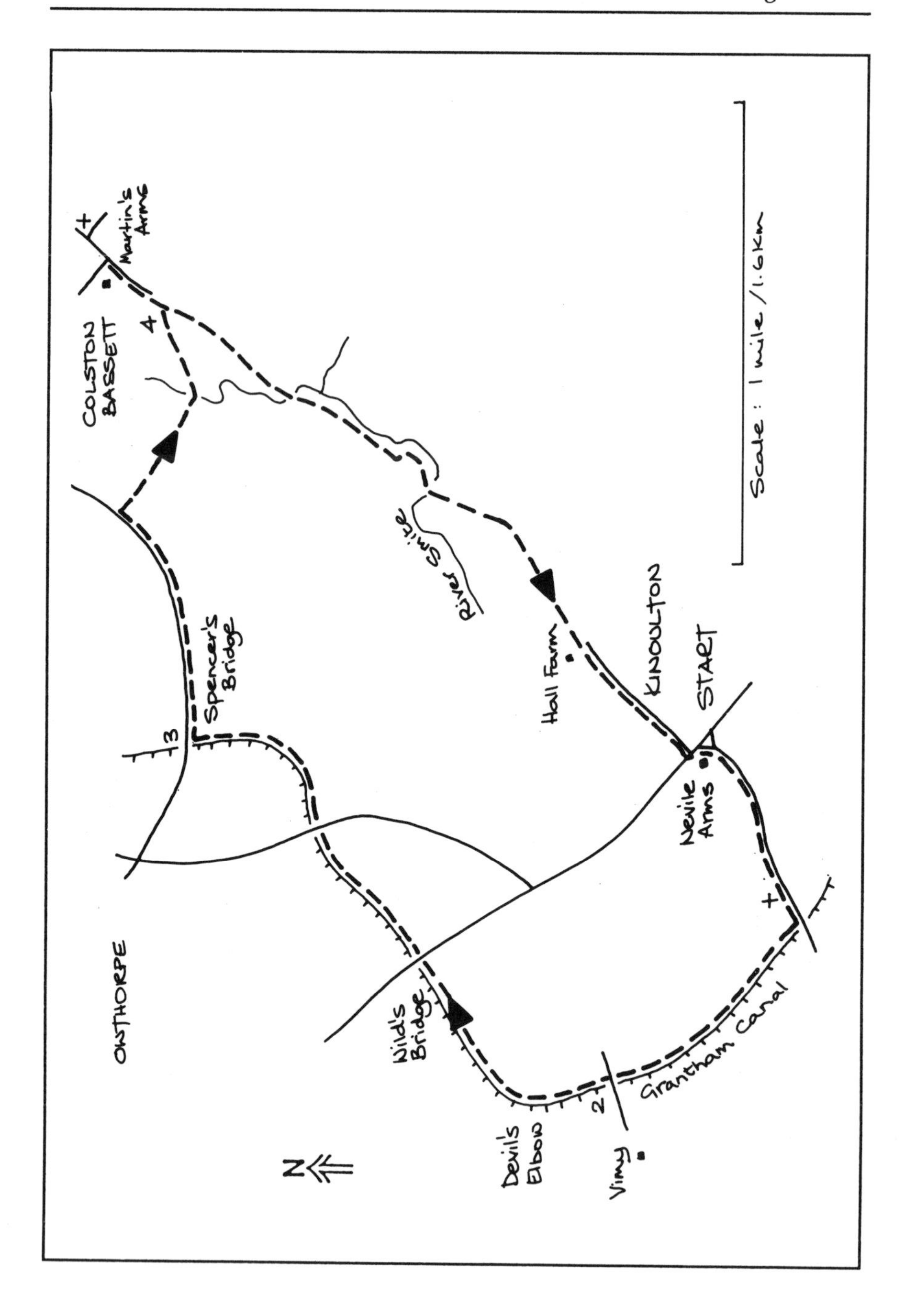
COLSTON BASSETT
Martin's Arms
4
River Smite
KINOULTON
Hall Farm
START
Nevile Arms
Spencer's Bridge
3
OWTHORPE
Wild's Bridge
Devil's Elbow
2
Grantham Canal
Vimy
N
Scale : 1 mile / 1.6km

(2) Continue along the towpath to Devil's Elbow and along a popular stretch to Wild's Bridge where there is a small parking area. Cross the road and continue ahead to cross the Cropwell road. The church seen on the hillside to the left is Owthorpe. To the right is a proposal for a major golf course development. This will alter the landscape and the quiet of these back lanes. The canal curves around to the left by a small nature reserve to Spencer's Bridge.

(3) Turn right here and walk along the Owthorpe road towards Colston Bassett. After the bend to the left, walk the length of the next straight stretch. Before the wood, go right through a gate and then ahead along a raised track that becomes greener and begins to curve gently left to a gate. Go through the wooden barred gate and head left towards the white houses at the edge of Colston Bassett village. Cross the stile by the gate and follow the track into the village and the Martins Arms.

(4) Retrace your steps along the lane that gives out to the track. Go ahead through a wicket gate by a double barred gate and ahead for approximately 100 metres to go through another gate. Walk through a lush meadow to a small gate by double gates and cross the concrete bridge over the infant River Smite, then through yet another wicket gate.

(5) The bridleway now follows the hedge on your left to the far top left corner of this very large field, alongside the river. The final part curves left and then right to a wooden bridge and barred gate. Once through, you can see Hall Farm ahead. Follow the hedge on the left but as it peels away to the left, head slightly left across the field towards the first electricity pole. The path is only slight on the ground in this field but, near the pole, cut right towards a gate in the direction of the farm. To the left and in the distance stands Hickling church.

(6) Go ahead through the gate and to another gate leading onto a road to the left of the farm. Walk ahead along this back road to Kinoulton passing by several sympathetic barn restorations. Pass the post office and stores to return to the Nevile Arms.

6. NORMANTON ON THE WOLDS

Route: Normanton on the Wolds – Clipston – Cotgrave Forest – Normanton/Plumtree

Distance: 5.5 miles

Map: O.S. Pathfinder 834 (Radcliffe on Trent & Keyworth)

Start: The Plough Public House, Normanton in the Wolds

(Grid Reference: SK 623327)

Access: Normanton in the Wolds lies just off the main A606 Melton Mowbray road, 6 miles to the South East of Nottingham. On street parking is available opposite the Plough, which serves Shipstones ales.

A regular bus service connects the Griffin Inn, Plumtree with Nottingham. The Griffin is a short walk from the Plough in Normanton. A less frequent bus service connects the Plough, Normanton with Nottingham. For travel details ring 0602 240000.

The Plough, Normanton-in-the-Wolds (0602 372401)

The Plough is a lovely old country pub with original old fine beams. Excellent Shipstones and Greenalls beers are served. Food is available Monday to Friday lunchtimes. Children are welcome in the large garden to the side. Note that this pub closes at 2.45pm Monday to Saturday lunchtimes, opening at 5.30pm Monday to Friday, and at 6.00pm on Saturday. Normal Sunday hours are observed.

The Griffin, Plumtree (0602 375743)

The Griffin at Plumtree is a large, but welcoming, Victorian local built in 1843. The modernised interior has a long central bar. Snacks and full meals are served every lunchtime and evening except Sunday. The

Griffin is open from 11am until 2.30pm on Mondays to Saturdays and from 5.30pm in the evening. There is an external children's play area and a welcoming garden. Excellent Kimberley Bitter and Classic are available from the only surviving independent Nottingham brewery.

Normanton on the Wolds

Normanton is a small rural community close to Tollerton Airfield; any light aircraft you see overhead will be flying to and from this small airfield. Normanton has excellent access to the City of Nottingham, yet enjoys a very enviable country setting. Farming and country pursuits form an important part of the life of this community.

The Griffin, Plumtree

The Walk

(1) The walk commences by The Plough public house in Normanton in the Wolds, off the A606 to Melton Mowbray. When facing the pub entrance, turn right along the road and walk towards the village centre. Be sure to look at the giant acorns on the gateway of a house to your right. Immediately past a yellow brick bungalow on your right, turn right over a wooden stile along a signposted footpath.

(2) At the end of the narrow lane, pass over a further stile, and follow the path straight on over the field. Keep to the left of the field. Proceed downhill to a double stile; pass over this stile and follow the path that continues rightwards. Cross a wooden footbridge over a stream, and follow the path that continues left. Go over a further stile; continue straight on along the path, noting the partially wooded Hoe Hill to your left. Follow the footpath through a grassy field, making for a stile at the left-hand end of the hedge at the edge of the field. Pass over two stiles to cross a lane, and the path continues straight ahead over a field that may contain horses. Pass over a bridge crossing a stream, and continue straight on along the path which leads directly over a field that may be ploughed. Cross a further footbridge at the end of this field, and continue along the path straight ahead and slightly left over afield which may be cropped, but where a distinct path line has been left. Pass over a stile at the end of this field and turn right along the road towards Clipston in the Wolds.

(3) Clipston in the Wolds is a small hamlet, sadly without a public house, but with several working farms. Walk through the village and, by Gilliver Cottage, at a junction, take the left-hand main road fork. Walk along the road, initially downhill, and then bear to the right. As the road bears left downhill, take the bridleway to your right through a metal gate, signposted R.U.P.P. Pass along this leafy lane, before keeping to the right-hand field margin. The path moves slightly downhill. The bridleway bears sharply right at the next field boundary. Turn right here, and keep to the right-hand edge of the field with the hedge directly on your right-hand side. The path now continues uphill. You have views over Cotgrave Village and Cotgrave Pit to your left. Join the lane at the end of the field, and continue slightly left and straight on along the path, which is now gravelled and leads towards Cotgrave Forest.

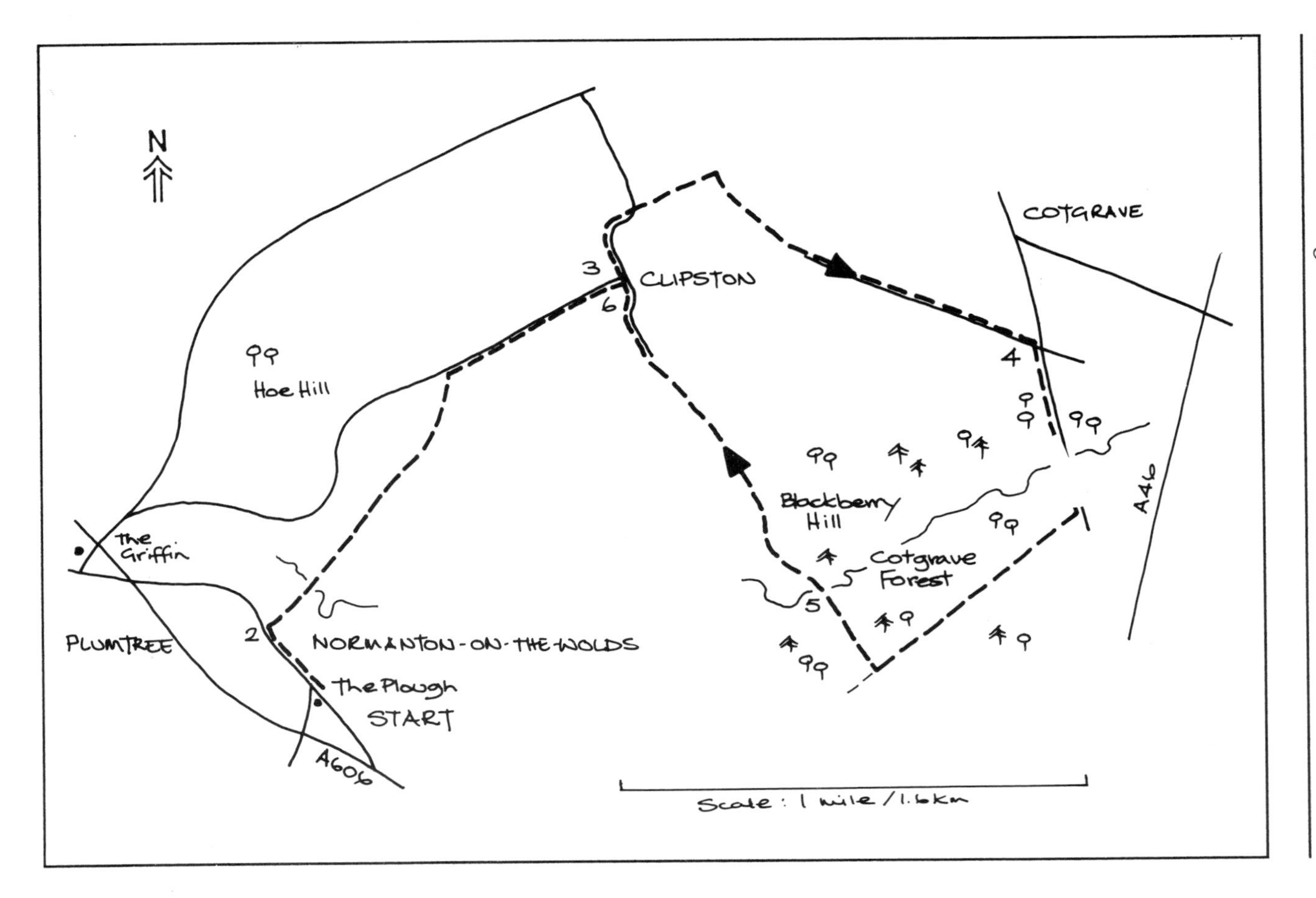
N
COTGRAVE
CLIPSTON
3
6
4
Hoe Hill
Blackberry Hill
Cotgrave Forest
A46
5
The Griffin
PLUMTREE
2
NORMANTON-ON-THE-WOLDS
The Plough
START
A606
Scale: 1 mile / 1.6km

(4) After three-quarters of a mile turn right at the bridleway crossroads, in front of the first trees of Cotgrave Forest. Follow a similar style of lane, which may be muddier as it goes gently downhill. Keep straight on with Cotgrave Forest to both sides. The path goes more steeply downhill. At the bottom of the hill, cross over a stream underneath power cables in a fire break. To your left lie the Cotgrave Wolds. The bridleway now climbs gently uphill. Beautiful butterflies and dragonflies can be seen along this path in late Summer. Turn right along the signposted bridleway at the crest of the hill. Pass through a wooden double-gated kind of stile/gate, and continue straight ahead along a wide gravelled road. Continue along this road as far as a further bridleway junction. Turn right here, and the roadway goes downhill. At the bottom of the hill, cross over the stream underneath the power lines, and begin your ascent of the bridleway.

(5) The path bears left around Blackberry Hill; it then turns rightwards and goes downhill. Pass out of Cotgrave Forest through a wooden gate/stile. Pass uphill along a wooded lane towards Clipston. Just before the village, bear with the path behind and to the right of a black barn. When you reach the main road, with Gilliver Cottage to your right and a post box opposite, turn left and retrace your steps to Normanton.

(6) Take care to bear left along the footpath over the fields upon leaving Clipston.

(7) Upon arrival back in Normanton, if you wish to visit The Griffin, in Plumtree, pass through the village of Normanton and cross the Melton Road, which brings you into Plumtree.

7. LANGAR

Route: Langar – Langar Lane – Colston Bassett – Langar

Distance: 4 miles

Map: O.S. Pathfinder 834 (Radcliffe on Trent and Keyworth)

Start: The Unicorns Head, Langar (Grid Reference: SK 724345)

Access: Langar is best approached by turning right on the A52 by pass at Bingham. The village is signposted off this road and there is limited on street car parking. Bartons provide a two hourly service to Langar from Nottingham except Sundays.

The Unicorns Head, Langar (0949 60460)

In true English fashion, bicycles are often stacked up beneath the awning of the outbuilding behind the pub as their owners partake of a pint in the extensive garden or public bar of the Unicorns Head. There's an aged AA sign on the wall of this old pub (date on the wall is 1717 AD) a feature of many hostelries in the Vale. This popular pub has a public bar on the left from the front entrance, and a lounge to the right. The bar is spacious and is well known for pub games and entertainment. Cask conditioned beers include Home mild and bitter, Theakstons Best Bitter and XB. Families are welcome and there is a large garden by the rear car park. Rolls are available during opening times: 11am until 2.30pm and 6pm in the evenings. Sunday lunchtime closing at 2.30 pm, otherwise standard hours prevail.

Langar

Langar stands on a slight edge which runs through the vale, known to the Anglo Saxons as The Lang and possible the derivation has been used to name the village. Besides the architectural merits of Langar Hall and the old rectory, the church is the most appealing structure in the village and is known as the "Cathedral of the Vale ". It contains many monuments and tombs to previous landowning families including the

Scrope family. One of these is mentioned in Shakespeare's series of Henry IV and V. A descendant of the Scrope family, Admiral Lord Howe, gained a place in textbooks for leading the relief of Gibraltar and the defeat of the French at the Battle of the Glorious First of June. He lies in the church. There are also monuments to the Chaworth family from Wiverton Hall just off the Bingham road.

The Unicorn's Head

The Walk

(1) From the Unicorn's Head, turn right to pass the village shop and houses. At the corner with a fine Georgian hall before you, turn left along Church lane to Langar church. The setting is decidedly rural with the church standing tall among trees, a school across a green and a barn complete with corrugated roof! The path is shown on the map as entering the churchyard and then turning left down to a green track. Most locals simply walk diagonally across the green to skirt the wall of the churchyard and ahead to cross a stile.

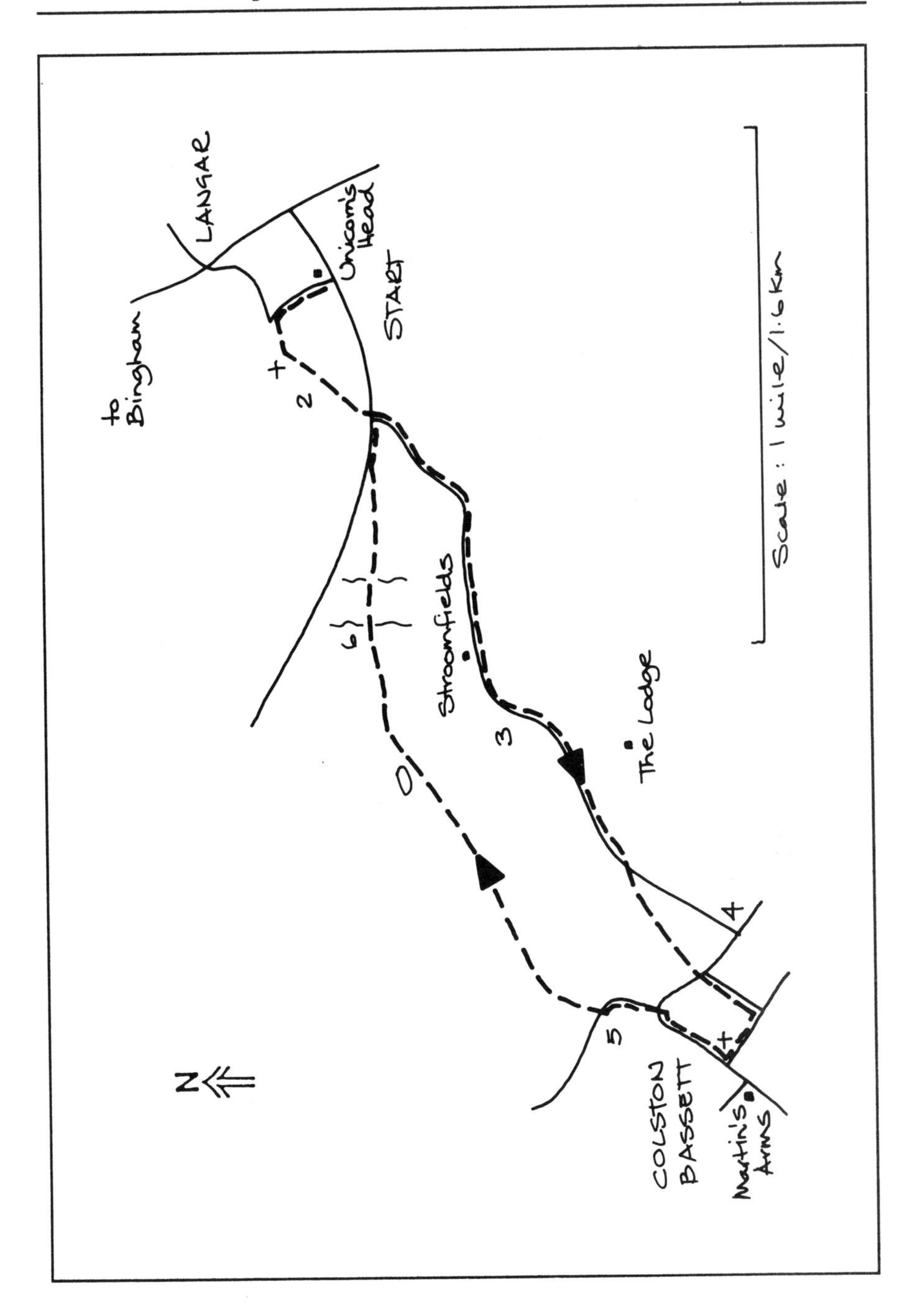
LANGAR
Unicorn's Head
START
to Bingham
2
6
Stroomfields
3
The Lodge
4
5
COLSTON BASSETT
Martin's Arms
N
Scale : 1 mile/1.6 Km

(2) There is a choice of two paths here. Head diagonally left along a worn path to the remains of a kissing gate and onto the road. Cross the road and bear left, noticing the old stone trough on the left. This lane follows passes through flat arable farming to what looks like a common, with the remains of ancient farming practices evidenced in the undulating furrows. Pass a house known as Stroon Fields and begin the slight rise to Colston Bassett, the church spire seen in the distance.

(3) The road widens, and a farm known as The Lodge is to the left. Just beyond a point parallel with the Lodge as the road bends gently right, look for double gates on the left and a barred gate on the right. Go through it and cross the stile on the left that can get a little overgrown in summer. Head diagonally right across the field in the direction of the church, but to the left of the houses. Exit at the gateway on to the road.

(4) Cross the road and walk up the lane almost opposite, bearing right at the junction for the church. The lane joins the main road. To the left is the old cross, post office and Martins Arms Inn, mentioned in the Kinoulton ramble. If not imbibing, cross the road, and turn right to walk up Church Gate. At the junction bear left along the Tithby and Bingham road.

(5) At the end house on the right go over a stile by a gate and walk ahead to go through another gate. Go straight on in the next field with a cricket pitch to the left. Go through the gap in the boundary ahead and cut across the next field in a similar direction. Cross a stile and proceed towards the top right corner passing to the right of a pool and Stroon Fields being a landmark across the fields to the right.

(6) Cross the stile and footbridge then bear right towards Langar, passing a hut in this next field before reaching another stile and footbridge. Keep ahead to cross another footbridge and stile mid field and then make your way to cut the corner of a field in the direction of the road. The final challenge is to cross another bridge that feels a little like walking the plank, climb up the embankment to cross the stile over the barrier and onto the road. Turn right to retrace your steps into Langar.

8. CROPWELL BISHOP

Route: Cropwell Bishop – Cropwell Butler – Cropwell Bishop

Distance: 3 miles (short route); 4 miles (longer route)

Map: O.S. Pathfinder 834 (Radcliffe on Trent & Keyworth)

Start: Wheatsheaf Inn, Cropwell Bishop (Grid Reference SK 684354)

Access: Cropwell Bishop is situated 10 miles South East of Nottingham; 1.5 miles East of the A46. The walk starts from the Wheatsheaf Inn; car parking is available opposite for patrons only. Limited on-street parking is available on Church Street opposite the Church of St. Giles, which dates in part from the 13th Century.

Cropwell Bishop is linked to Nottingham by a regular hourly bus service. (0602 240000).

The Wheatsheaf Inn, Cropwell Bishop (0602 892247)

This beautiful pub is a 400 year old coaching inn. It is thought that Dick Turpin stayed at one of the pubs in the village, to be close to the lucrative traffic on the Fosse Way. The Wheatsheaf serves a fine range of real ales: Home mild and bitter, Theakstons XB and Youngers No 3. Food is served at lunchtimes and evenings. The Wheatsheaf is open noon until 3pm on Mondays to Fridays except Wednesdays, and from 6pm in the evening. The pub is open all day on Saturdays and usual Sunday hours prevail. Families are welcomed, and an outdoor drinking area/garden is available.

The Plough Inn, Cropwell Butler (0602 333124)

This pleasant village local serves the following real ales: Home bitter, Theakstons XB and Theakstons Old Peculier. It serves food every lunchtime and evening, excepting Sunday evening. A separate children's room is available, and there is also an outdoor drinking area/garden. The Plough is open from Mondays to Fridays from mid-day until 3pm and re-opens at 6.30pm in the evenings. Usual Sunday hours apply.

Cropwell Bishop

Cropwell Bishop is a typically attractive South Nottinghamshire rural community. The Church of St. Giles is particularly fine and dates back to 1215. Some farming activity survives in the area, but the local populace relies mainly on commuting to Nottingham for employment.

The Walk

(1) When facing the Wheatsheaf Inn from the car park opposite, turn right and walk along road. Note the Wesleyan Chapel on the left, and the Cropwell Bishop Creamery to your right. Take the footpath to the right that lies just before a bus stop, and opposite Kinoulton Road to the left. The footpath initially runs between new housing on the right and a children's playground on the left. You will see the wooded Hoe Hill ahead and to the left.

(2) Keep to the path on the right-hand edge of the field. At the end of the field follow the path to the right and keep the fence and housing directly to your right. The footpath here is enclosed between a barbed wire fence to the left and a stream to the right. It continues along the right-hand edge of the next field. Ignore the stile to the right, and continue straight on through a wooden gate. Keep to the right-hand edge of the field; Hoe Hill lies now to your left; cross over a footpath, ignoring a further stile to your right. Keep the hedge directly to your right. The path now descends slightly, as you leave Hoe Hill behind and to your left.

(3) Pass through gates and continue onwards along a wide grassy footpath hedged on both sides. The path now starts to go uphill a little. Ignore the grassy path to the left, and continue straight along the path, bearing to the right. After 50 yards, take the stile on your right. The path leads diagonally left across a field towards modern housing with a red roof. A narrow path leads to the left of this housing at the end of the field. Cross over the stile, and you find yourself in Cropwell Butler.

(4) Turn right along the road, keeping to the left of the post box and the salt box. At the end of Back Lane, follow the Main Road straight ahead; this leads to the Plough Inn (Home Ales) which is straight ahead on the

left-hand side of the road. This pub has a beer garden. There are bus-stops 20 yards before the Plough Inn. Note the public garden to the right beyond the Plough. Admire the many fine houses and gardens. The road bears to the left. Take the road to the left just before the village pump and bus shelter. Ignore Back Lane to the left and continue straight on. There is a fascinating thatched cottage on the left, with thatched animals carved into the roof. Opposite the Old Police House on the edge of the village, take the public bridleway over the field to the left.

(5) Keep the hedge immediately to your left, and disregard the footpath that leads diagonally across the field. Go left over the footbridge and through the gate at the end of the field. Continue straight on, keeping the hedge to your right. Go through the wooden gate. Turn right and then immediately left up the bridleway. Hoe Hill is visible to the right on the horizon. The bridleway gently runs uphill, before descending and passing the path on the left that you previously took to Cropwell Butler. You can now continue along the bridleway and retrace your steps to Cropwell Bishop, or take the alternative longer route around Hoe Hill.

LONGER ALTERNATIVE ROUTE

(6) Take the bridleway off to the right; this is marked by a blue waymarker post on the right, and is initially a wide grassed path, starting just before a metal gate on the right. Keep the hedge on your left until it disappears, and then follow the bridleway straight across a field that may be ploughed or cropped. Make for the wooden bridleway post that lies straight across the field ahead of you, beneath the highest of a clump of trees. When you have reached the edge of the field and the public bridleway signpost, continue straight on keeping the hedge and a pond to your left.

(7) The path bears to the left and through a white wooden gate. Walk straight on, keeping to the right-hand edge of the field. At the gate/gateway where the bridleway continues, bear up left towards a stile. At the stile turn around to face the way you have come, and follow the towpath on your side of the disused canal. If, instead, you wish to enjoy a picnic, note the tables and benches by the disused canal lock.

The Grantham Canal does not have a particularly romantic history, as it was mainly used to transport night soil from towns and cities, most

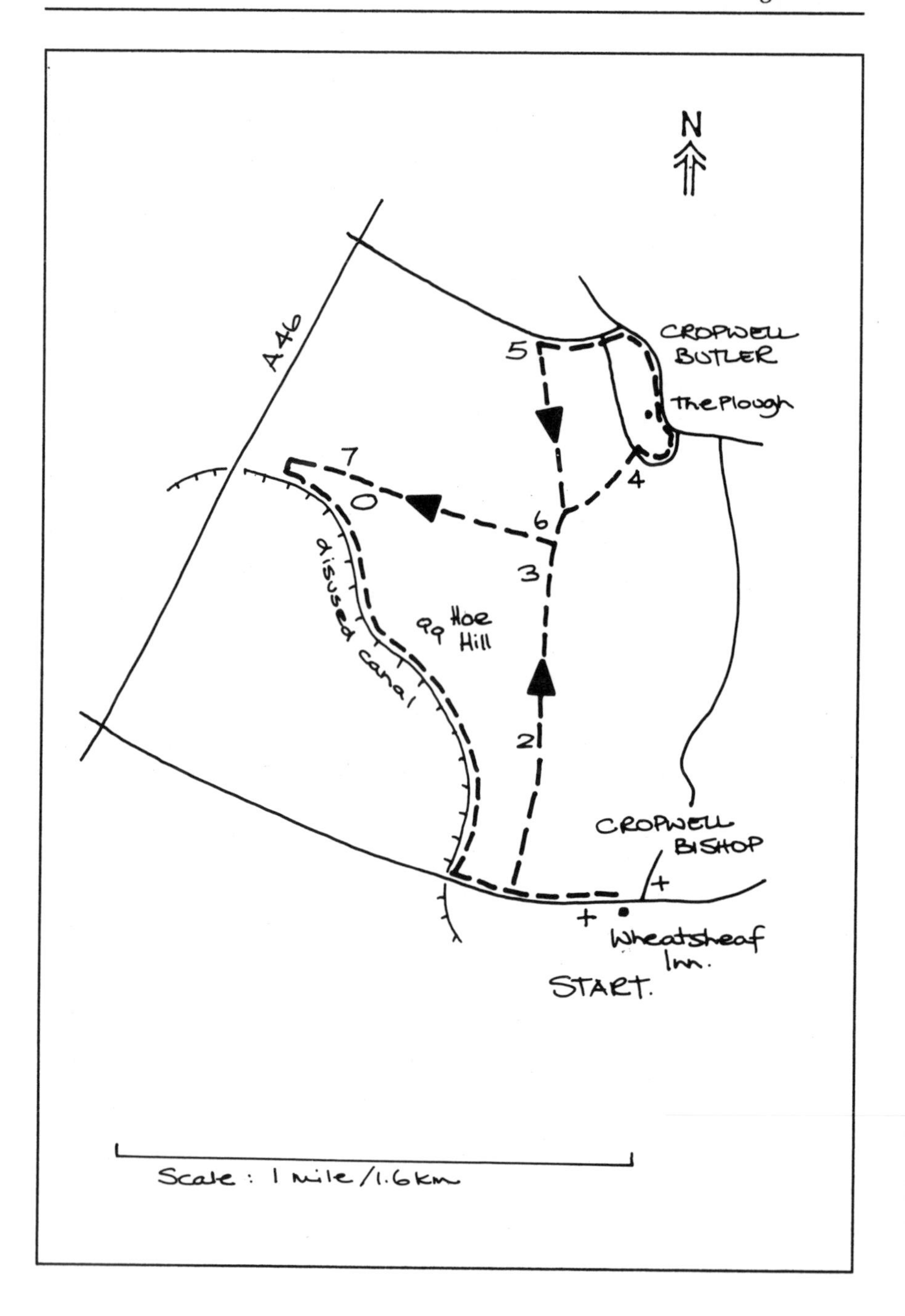
N
A46
CROPWELL BUTLER
The Plough
5
4
7
6
3
2
disused canal
99 Hoe Hill
CROPWELL BISHOP
Wheatsheaf Inn.
START.
Scale: 1 mile/1.6km

especially from Nottingham, to be used as manure on the fertile fields. Note the variety of disused bridges and canal marker posts. Follow the canal towpath along the left-hand of the bank that returns you to Cropwell Bishop through a succession of stiles. The path may be overgrown in places. The towpath on the right-hand side of the canal is owned by the British Waterways Board, and may be used by walkers, but is not a guaranteed right of way.

(8) After about a mile, cut through a hedge into a children's playground, again keeping the canal to your right. Cross over the gate onto the road, and turn left to return to the Wheatsheaf Inn. If you turn left into Church Street, the Chequers Inn (Theakstons Ales) lies 50 metres further along on your right.

The Grantham Canal, Vale of Belvoir

9. GRANBY

Route: Granby – Grantham Canal – Plungar – Barkestone-le-Vale – Granby

Distance: 6 miles

Map: O.S. Pathfinder 834 (Radcliffe-on-Trent & Keyworth)

Start: The Boot and Shoe Inn, Granby (Grid Reference: SK 748362)

Access: Granby is in the heart of the Vale of Belvoir. Travel on the A52 road towards Grantham turning right at The Haven and right again at the first crossroads. There is limited on street parking in the village. Bartons run a two hourly service throughout the week but not on Sundays. Contact the Bartons/Trent busline on (0332) 292200 for details.

The Boot and Shoe Inn, Granby (0949 50354)

The lively free house tucked away at edge of the village offers a warm welcome to the walker. The public bar area is both traditional and homely with a smarter lounge to the left of the entrance. Jennings Mild and Marstons Pedigree are usually on handpull but there is also a continuing range of guest beers available. Food is served during opening times and there is also an outdoor drinking area. Families are welcome. The Boot and Shoe is open from noon until 2pm (extended to 4pm on Saturdays) and from 5.30pm each evening. Usual Sunday opening.

Granby

The narrow streets of Granby allow access to huddled old red brick cottages of the last century which give an impression that this was a small township in earlier times. Most would have been employed in agriculture and some small scale quarrying but Granby never really grew beyond a population of 500 and has since declined during the past century. The key institutions survive, the church with a magnificent tower, post office and two public houses, the other being The Marquis of Granby, the name reflecting an earlier Duke of Rutland's title.

Plungar

Plungar is an equally pleasant village lying just over the Leicestershire border where a settlement nestles around the smaller church. Near the village is "Our Little Farm", a working farm open to the public from Spring to Autumn (Tel: 0949 60349).

Belvoir Castle, the seat of the Duke of Rutland, can be seen several miles away, described by more than one author as the perfect romantic castle. The parks, gardens, and parts of the castle housing considerable treasures are also open to the public.

The Church, Barkestone-le-Vale

The Walk

(1) Turn right from the entrance road to the Boot and Shoe public house to walk to the crossroads by the church. Go right and walk along the road in the direction of Plungar, passing the fine building of Manor farm. The road begins a long and straight section at a small bridge over a water course. Look for a footpath signposted through a gap in the hedge on the left. Then walk ahead to join the bank of the stream and proceed along the edge of the field, the spire of Barkestone church ahead.

(2) Towards the far corner of the field cross a red brick bridge over the water channel and bear right to follow the field's edge to a gap leading onto a track. Go left here but then bear almost immediately right through a barred gate (path signpost here). Walk ahead through the first pasture with the water channel still to the right. Go through a gap in the next boundary and then head left away from the water to the next hedge of hawthorn bushes. Pass through a gap again and head in a similar direction to cross a stile. Bear half-left in the next field almost in line towards Barkestone-le-Vale church. Find the footbridge in the hedge between rosehip bushes and climb up steps to the track once again.

(3) Turn right and follow this lonely track to the bridge over the old railway track that ran from near Bottesford to Melton Mowbray and then up to the Grantham Canal, restored by the Grantham Canal Restoration Society. The slight rise above the flat landscape around allows a good view back to Granby, the impressive church tower being a landmark throughout this part of the Vale. The way down to the canal is to the left. Then turn to walk under the bridge and along the towpath. Pass the information board and mileage post indicating 21 miles to the Trent.

(4) At the next bridge, climb up to road level again and go left into the village. On the right is a local butchers and Grange Farm pottery. At the staggered crossroads turn left into Church lane, unless calling in at the Belvoir Inn which offers a real ale or two and bed and breakfast. Pass the tidy little Wesleyan chapel on the left, dating from 1874, and as the road swings left go right along a path that cuts off in front of the entrance gates to Manor Home farm. Turn left at the road to pass by Plungar church.

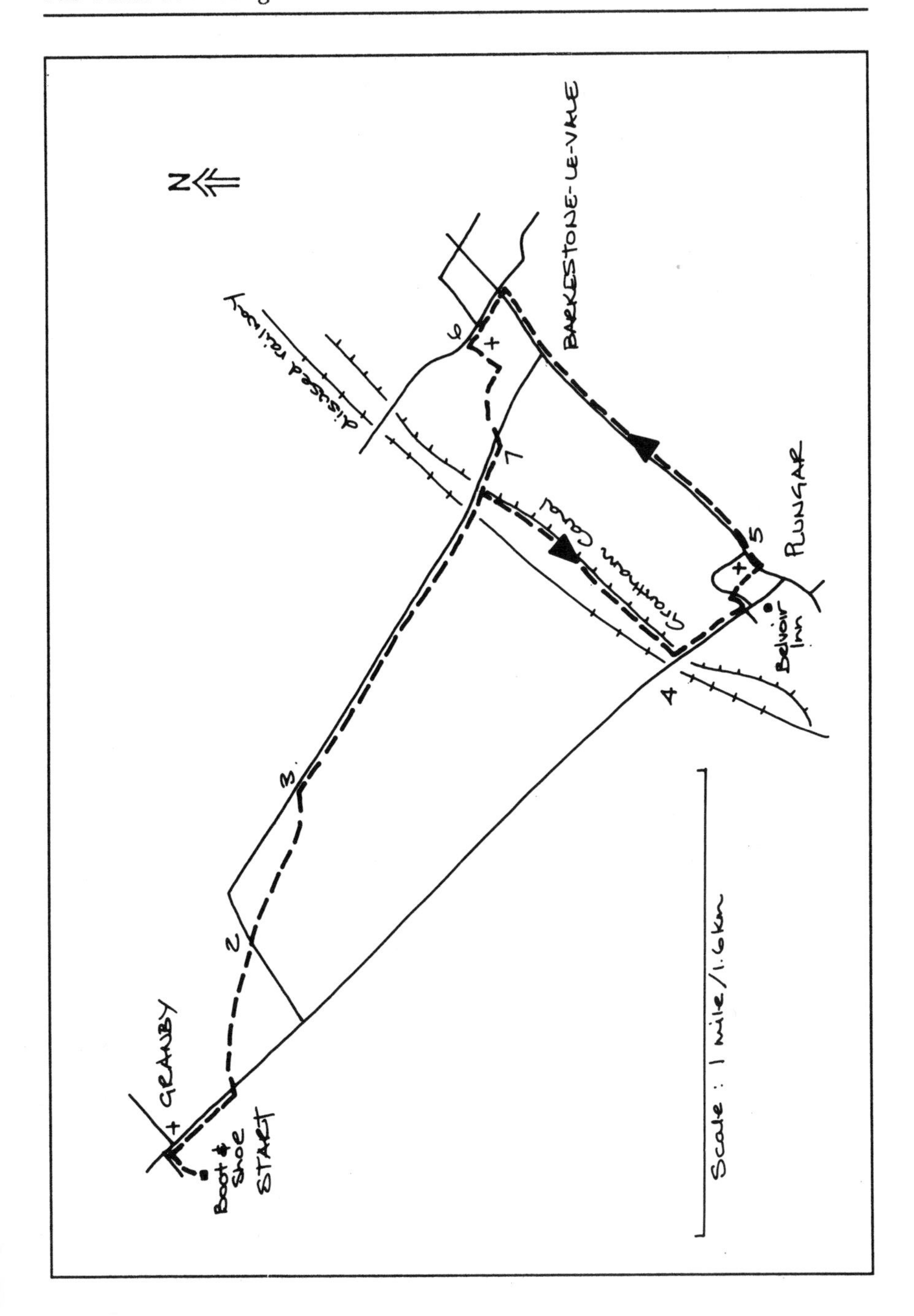
N
BARKESTONE-LE-VALE
disused railway
Grantham Canal
PLUNGAR
Belvoir Inn
GRANBY
Boot & Shoe
START
Scale : 1 mile/1.6km
1
2
3
4
5
6

(5) The straight road to Barkestone-le-Vale is lightly trafficked, not particularly inspiring, but does have the redeeming quality of views over to Redmile and Belvoir Castle. On entering Barkestone, there's also a good view across the field to the parish church, one of the many historic churches of the Vale. At the crossroads, turn left by the old school into Jericho Lane. Before turning, take a look at the oval slate tablet dating from 1814 that recognises the kind sponsorship by Daniel Smith to help in the education of 26 poor children in the neighbourhood including an

"Endowment of £15 per annum for ever to Vicar and Church Wardens (for the time being)".

Those seeking refreshment might like to turn right at the crossroads and go along Middle Street to the Chequers public house in Rutland Square.

(6) Pass by the gateway to the church and at the end of the churchyard go left over a stile and walk ahead to cross another stile into a field. Keep ahead to cross the next stile and then bear right to proceed along the field's edge to cross another stile just to the left of the corner. Head slightly left across the field to a signpost where a stile exits onto a track by the canal again.

(7) Go right and follow the track back to the point where the steps lead down to the footbridge into the field. Retrace your steps back to Granby as walked in the outward section.

10. ASLOCKTON

Route: Aslockton – Blackberry Hill – Orston – River Smite – Aslockton

Distance: 4 miles

Map: O.S. Pathfinder 813 (Carlton and Elston)

Start: The Cranmer Arms, Aslockton (Grid reference: SK 742401)

Access: Aslockton is just off the A52 Nottingham to Grantham road. There is a limited bus service to nearby Whatton but a much better daily train service to Aslockton on the Nottingham to Grantham line. There is limited car parking near Aslockton railway station.

The Cranmer Arms, Aslockton (0949 50362)

Nearly twenty years ago the local CAMRA guide described the Cranmer as a "homely village pub" and thankfully this is just how it is today. Two areas are served by one bar bedecked with several handpulls serving Home Mild and Bitter, Younger and Theakston bitters from the Scottish and Newcastle stable. The unusual, probably unique, name of the pub refers to Archbishop Cranmer mentioned below. He left the village before reaching drinking age, if there happened to be one in the fifteenth century, and remained abstemious throughout his eventful existence. Food is offered at the Cranmer Arms on Thursday to Sunday lunchtimes and there is a large beer garden suitable for families at the rear. The Cranmer is open 11am until 3pm Mondays to Fridays and from 7pm in the evenings. It is open all day Saturdays. Usual Sunday opening.

The Durham Ox, Orston (0949 50059)

This splendid village local stands opposite the church under shade of churchyard trees. There are two tie-rings outside the pub, one for horses, the other for ferrets! Inside is an L shaped room around a bar, the section on the right being more of a bar area with several traditional pub games on offer. Home Bitter, Theakstons Best and Theakstons XB are available on handpull and rolls and hot pies too throughout opening times. Opening times are: 12 until 3pm Mondays to Saturdays, 6pm evening opening, 6.30pm on Saturdays. Usual Sunday opening. Well behaved families are welcome at lunchtime and early evening, and there is an outdoor drinking area. The hosts describe the Durham Ox as "just an old fashioned English pub". Long may it survive.

Aslockton

Aslockton is a pleasant little village on the right or wrong side of the railway tracks, depending on how you view it. On the other side of the tracks is Whatton and since the last century the railway has been a dividing line between these two pleasant rural settlements. Both grew up as farming communities but tend now to be dominated by villagers travelling to Nottingham or Grantham for employment.

Aslockton is best known for being the birthplace of Archbishop Cranmer in 1489. At 14 he was despatched to Cambridge to reach scholarly heights before pursuing a career in the clergy. As an Archdeacon he was consulted by Henry VIII in the divorce of Catherine of Aragon. Good king Henry was so pleased with Cranmer's resistance to the Pope's objections that the Archdeacon was elevated to the highest of earthly positions, Archbishop of Canterbury. In this job he played a leading role in the establishment of Protestantism in England becoming one of the leading figures during the Reformation. Twenty years later, however, Queen Mary demanded allegiance to the Catholic faith and Cranmer was burnt to the stake in 1554 for his dissenting beliefs.

Orston

The village has been for the most part a self sufficient agricultural community. It almost made the grade as a spa resort in the last century for the waters here are rich in chalybeate. This was not to be. Instead, a less glamorous activity, the mining of gypsum, took hold of the community until the 1870s when the local company ceased trading.

The Walk

(1) From the entrance of the Cranmer Arms turn left to pass by another good pub, The Old Greyhound, which is also recommended by the authors. Cross the tracks and turn immediately left to go through a kissing gate. The coralled path soon joins another coming in from the left. Turn right along a metalled path and walk over the bridges towards Whatton church. To the right are the scant earthwork remains of a fish pond probably dating from medieval times. The church dates from the middle ages and it is along this path that Cranmer no doubt ran by his father's side to worship each day.

(2) The path joins a road by the church, then passes the old vicarage to a junction. Turn left along Chapel walk, beyond the Wesleyan chapel dating from 1846 and to a narrow path between gardens and by the entrance to Manor farm. Proceed ahead on the track which keeps to the left of a barn. At the time of writing it looked as if this area might well be primed for development. The track bends gently left to a bridge (although the tractor bridge to the left is far safer). Walk straight ahead to a stile which is crossed and then head over the brow of Blackberry hill, although there is little chance of finding blackberries for now this field is mainly in cereal crop. The way is not clear but it should lead over the brow of the hillock towards a pylon and then descend to an underbridge at the railway. Locals tend to use a track that skirts the perimeter of this field on the right and then left to the same point at the railway.

(3) Go through the railway underbridge. Bear slightly right in the next field keeping to the right of the nearest pylon and through a line of hawthorns. An old sleeper bridge marks the spot. The path then bears left following the dried up old water course on the left to meet a ditch and hedge. Go left towards the River Smite and then right to follow the river bank towards Orston. As the village is approached the riverside path bears right, following a drainage ditch to a tractor bridge. Ironically, there is an old sleeper bridge to the left here and a new wooden bridge on the right. The way proceeds up to a barred gate. Immediately beyond it, turn left to walk along a leafy lane into the village.

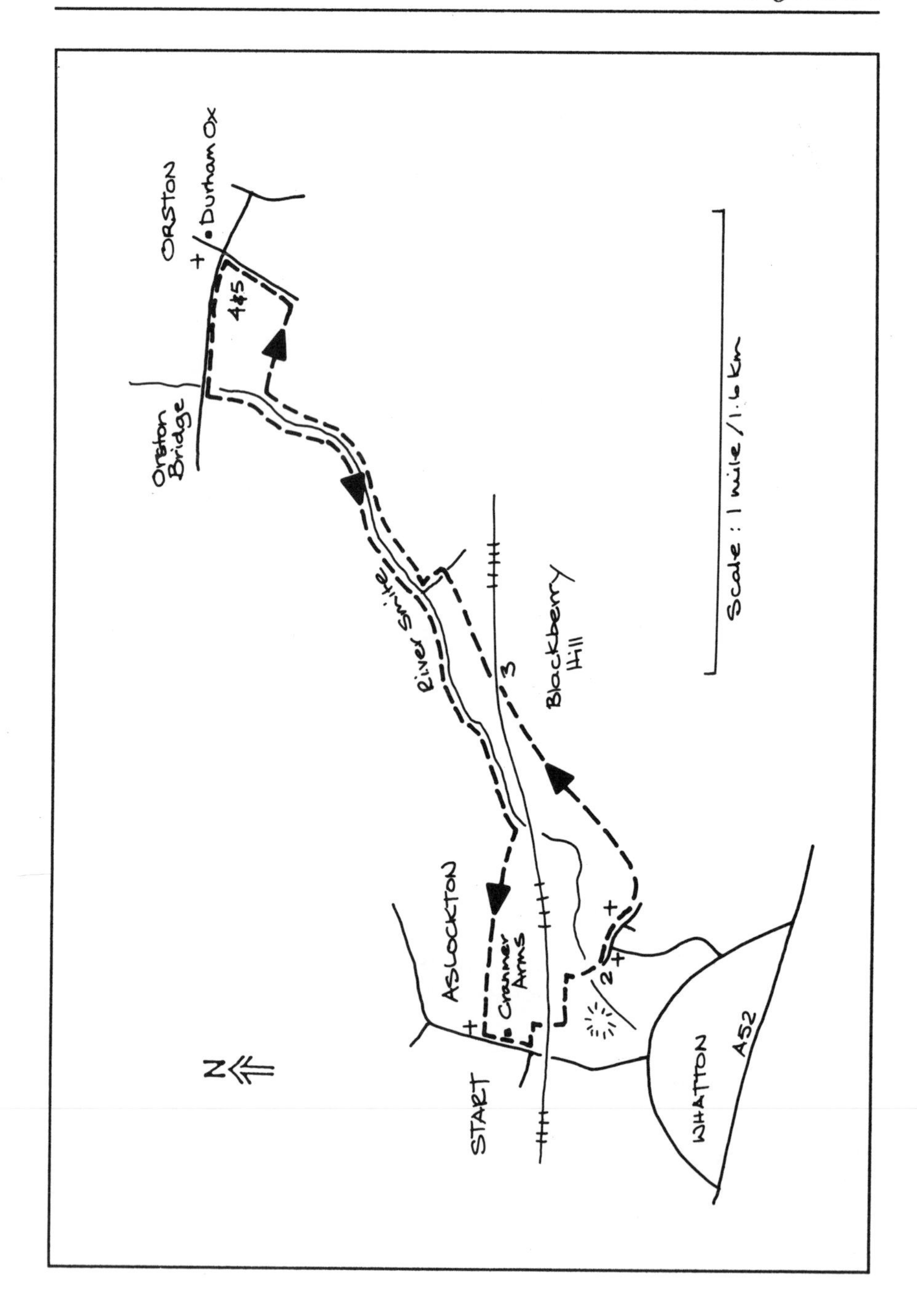
ORSTON
Durham Ox
4&5
Orston Bridge
River Smite
3
Blackberry Hill
Scale : 1 mile / 1.6 Km
ASLOCKTON
Cranmer Arms
2
START
WHATTON
A52
N

(4) At the crossroads the church stands almost opposite, a pretty stone building dating from medieval times but much restored through the centuries. To the right of God's Acre, stands the Durham Ox.

(5) Turn left at the crossroads and leave the village by way of Orston Bridge over the River Smite. Go left here, as signposted, along a well-worn path on the far bank of the river. The way is straightforward, following for the best part the watercourse back to Aslockton. Fifty metres before the railway bridge, over the river the path veers half-right with the hedge on your left. Follow the hedge to the end of the field, through a gap. Ten metres after, the path veers to the right in the corner of the field, cross a plank over the ditch and then cross the stile and walk ahead to join a track that brings you to a gateway. Veer half-right and continue on the track around the farm to reach the road in the village, having passed (on the right) the remains of Cranmer's mound, most probably a motte and bailey dating from earlier centuries than Cranmer's lifetime. Cranmer almost certainly walked these fields as a boy, as his home would have been in close proximity.

On the right, just before reaching the road, is the Church of St Thomas. Once on the road turn left to The Cranmer Arms, to ponder, perhaps, on the significance of standing up for one's beliefs.

11. KIMBERLEY (SWINGATE)

Route: Swingate – Strelley Home Farm – Cossall – Nottingham Canal – Cossall Marsh – Strelley Park Farm – Swingate

Distance: 6 miles

Map: O.S. Pathfinder 812 Nottingham North

Start: Layby opposite White Lion, Swingate (Grid Reference SK 502439)

Access: There is a daily bus services to Swingate from Kimberley. Travel on the A610 to junction with A6096, follow signs for Kimberley. In Kimberley turn right at the mini roundabout, then left by the school. Follow this road to the White Lion.

Kimberley

KImberley is a quiet little Nottinghamshire town, well known to beer enthusiasts as the home of KImberley ales from Hardys and Hansons plc. The names reflect two breweries that stood on opposite sides of the road in the town. Ironically, these one-time competitors shared the same water supply. The existing brewery is still controlled by descendants of the Hardy and Hansons families.

The Queen Adelaide, Swingate (0602 383184)

The Queen Adelaide is a welcoming public house serving Hardys and Hansons beers, a pub described in a previous Good Beer Guide as having a "social club-like atmosphere". It is open Mondays to Saturdays from 11am until 2.30pm (3pm on Saturdays), reopening at 5.30pm in the evening.

Usual Sunday hours. There is an outdoor area and families are welcome. The landlord suggests that the pub was originally a factory so the building really has changed use.

The Queen Adelaide

The Walk

(1) From the White Lion go right at the telephone box along Babbington Lane. Before you reach the water tower and tantalisingly close to the entrance to the Queen Adelaide, go left along the footpath signed to Strelley. This crosses the pub car park and then runs tightly enclosed by fence and hedge to reach the road.

(2) At the road go straight ahead down the track, waymarked and signed as a bridleway. This soon enters open fields, with the TV booster station to the left. The track soon splits three ways. Take the middle course by the blue and yellow post. Swingate Farm lies to the right and ahead you can see Windmill Farm, though of the windmill itself there is no trace.

A dull rumble can now be discerned, partly felt, partly heard. It is, of course, the all pervading noise of the M1, which is only two fields away, though hidden at this point in a cutting. There is a good view to the right, over Spring Wood across the Erewash Valley to Ilkeston.

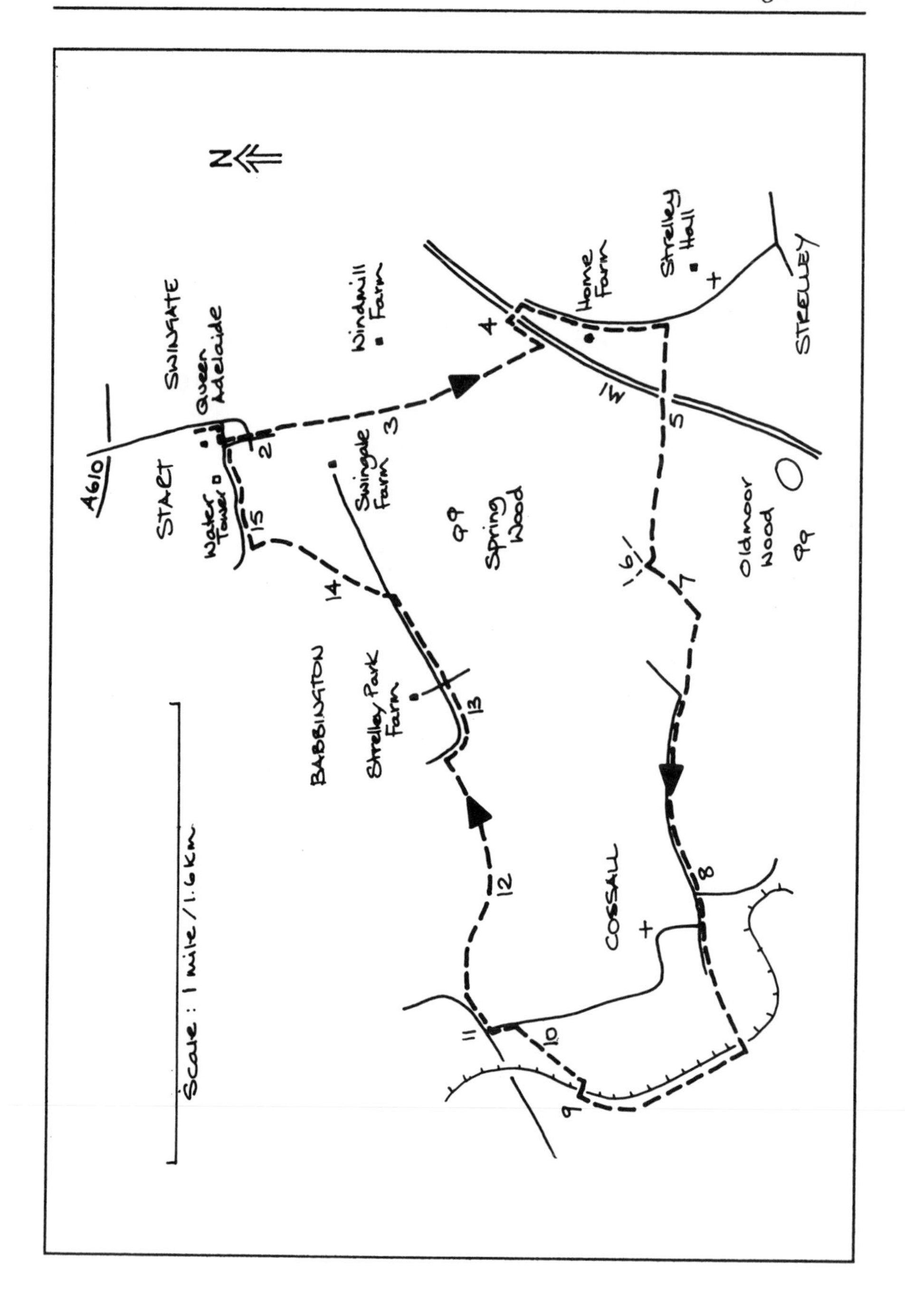
N
A610
START
Water Tower
Queen Adelaide
SWINGATE
Swingate Farm
Spring Wood
Windmill Farm
Home Farm
Strelley Hall
STRELLEY
M1
Oldmoor Wood
BABBINGTON
Strelley Park Farm
COSSALL
2
3
4
5
6
7
8
9
10
11
12
13
14
15
Scale : 1 mile / 1.6 km

(3) Where the track goes left to Windmill Farm, carry straight on along the path, which is signposted. The path is constrained by a fence to the left and a hedge to the right, but soon comes to another gateway and junction of tracks. The M1 can now be seen ahead, along with the bridge that takes you over to Strelley. It is tempting to make a bee-line across the field to the bridge. Naughty! The right of way follows the right-hand edge of the field, then turns sharp left at the M1 and follows the boundary fence of the motorway to the bridge.

(4) Cross the bridge and bear right at the far side, down the track. At the gateway by Home Farm, continue straight on along what is now a tarred road. The grounds of Strelley Hall are on the left and apart from the motorway rumble, this a very pleasant little village. Opposite the main entrance to Strelley Hall, go right, through a gate, which is signed as a footpath. The track immediately splits four ways. Three have gates and are private. The fourth has no gate and is your route. The hedged lane soon reaches the motorway and crosses it on another bridge. If you can bring yourself to stop on the bridge, the view south is quite good and very extensive. Just over the bridge on the left, is Oldmoor Pond.

(5) Carry on along the lane, ignoring paths going off to the right, most of which aren't shown on the OS map. The spire of Cossall church is ahead and the track seems to be making straight for it. Where the track forks three ways, go straight ahead. This part of the walk is along a classic green lane separated from the surrounding fields by fences and hedges.

(6) There is a gradual descent, at the bottom of which the lane bears right. The OS map shows a path going off to the left, cutting across the field corner. The finger post is at the opposite side of the field, but there is no stile at your end. Anyhow, this is one of those instances where the length of time taken to negotiate two stiles would be greater than walking round on the bridleway. Don't be a purist, but follow the lane to the junction and then turn left to reach the cottage.

(7) At the cottage the lane ceases, but a footpath carries straight on, over a signposted stile, into fields. Keep by the hedge on the left to another stile, at which point the spire of Cossall church is in view again. The OS map shows the path making a diagonal line across this field, but in practice the path keeps by the left-hand side, to a stile in a new-ish fence. At this point bear right, keeping to the right of the solitary tree, heading

towards the houses of Cossall and the far right-hand corner of the field. The approach to the exit stile is very muddy, but mercifully this is soon over and the path emerges onto Robinetts Lane just alongside a seat. Go left here along the lane, (the Robinetts Arm of the former Nottingham Canal is down to the left), and thus reach the main road through Cossall.

(8) At the main road, go straight ahead towards the village. Where the road goes sharp right, just beyond the curious cut-away house on the left, cross over (taking great care) then go down Mill Lane, signposted to the canal. The lane is little more than a broad path as it descends towards the Erewash Valley. Across the valley is Ilkeston. The canal is soon reached, but the bridge carrying Mill Lane over the cut has been demolished and the canal culverted. Go right here, along the towpath, which is in a good state of repair. Indeed the canal looks almost fit for traffic at this point. An easy level walk follows, with newly planted woodland to the left and fields leading up to Cossall on the right. On the opposite side of the valley is Ilkeston, and the rival Erewash Canal. There was a celebrated dispute when the Nottingham Canal was built about who owned the water in the River Erewash, from which both companies drew their supplies. Despite many protestations the Erewash fed both throughout their commercial existence. The side of the canal is alive with birds, including various ducks, coot and long tailed tits.

(9) At the first bridge, again not a traditional canal structure, go right, cross the canal and then follow the waymarked path round to the left. It is signed to Cossall Marsh. This path is not shown on the OS map but is part of the Nottingham Canal Trail. Ahead on the top of the hill can be seen the water tower at Swingate. All that now remains is to climb back up to it!

(10) The path proceeds through rough fields with the canal on the left, before swinging right to a stile. The stile takes you out onto the road and here you go left, down to the T junction. To the left the canal spans the road, but your route now leaves the canal behind for good and goes right, along Awsworth Lane.

(11) Awsworth Lane is a main road, despite its name, so it is with relief that you locate the footpath on the right, just where the road bears left. The path is signposted and runs down the side of a brown house to a footbridge over a small stream. Once over the stream and in the field, go left by the hedge to reach another footbridge over a well hidden ditch.

This is closely followed by a stile. Once over the stile go right, following the hedge up towards the multi armed signpost seen ahead.

(12) At the signpost, cross the stile on the route signed to Kimberley and Strelley. The path here is almost a track and is easy to follow. A gateway in the field corner carries the track into the next field. Still keep the hedge to your right until the far corner is reached. Here there are two stiles, but you ignore the one in the right-hand hedge and proceed straight ahead. Pass through the next field, still keeping the hedge to your right to find a further stile that emerges into a narrow rough lane, signposted to Strelley. Go right here, vowing to return to pick the harvest of sloes and wondering where your illicit still has gone to.

(13) The land broadens and bends left to reveal Strelley Park Farm on the left. This is a curious and not too successful mixture of building styles. At the "crossroads" go straight on, ignoring footpath signs shortly afterwards, and proceeding instead along the stony track. The track now begins to rise towards Swingate Farm, but here there is a sign showing that the route ahead is private. On the left however, is a signpost directing you over a stile and into the field. Once in the field, bear right and head towards the mast seen on the horizon. To the left lies Babbington and the former colliery site, now completely vanished.

(14) The stile taking you out of this field is mid-way along the hedge, in direct line with the mast. In the next field continue up the hill in the same direction, with a surprising view left to Crich Stand and Alport Hill. The remains of a former field boundary are crossed, then the path, still making for the mast, reaches a signpost in the far hedge. Here the route goes left, along a very narrow, hedged path. On the right the land rises quite steeply into gardens. To the left are the fields. The path struggles out of the undergrowth, through an arch of thorn, to reach a lane.

(15) At the lane go right and ascend the final few feet of the hill, past the bungalows until the mast and Swingate water tower come into view. For all its utilitarian function, the water tower is quite an attractive building, obviously an object of civic pride when it was built by Nottingham Water Works. The view from the top must be very fine indeed.

A quick sprint past the tower brings you to the Queen Adelaide again and thus to the end of the walk.

12. FLINTHAM

Route: Flintham – Syerston – Elston – Sibthorpe – Flintham

Distance: 5 miles

Map: O.S. Pathfinder 813 (Carlton and Elston)

Start: Boot and Shoe Public House, Flintham (Grid Reference SK 742260)

Access: Flintham lies half a mile to the East of the A46, 12 miles to the North East of Nottingham. Ample on-street parking is available outside the Boot and Shoe, and there is a car park behind the pub for patrons.

A regular hourly bus service connects Nottingham with Newark, which serves a bus-stop on the main A46, leaving a short walk to the centre of Flintham.

The Boot and Shoe, Flintham (0636 525246)

The Boot and Shoe is a fine country inn with a wealth of curiosities, such as the histories of the nearby RAF bases of Syerston and Newton, displayed on the walls of the lounge. The wall of an out-building in the car park contains a large beehive of masonry bees that can be seen in full activity in late Spring and early Summer. The landlord assures the authors that these bees do not sting! The Boot and Shoe currently serves Home Ales under pressure, but traditional real ale is to be introduced shortly. Meals are available every lunchtime and evening except for Sunday evening. The Boot and Shoe is open from 11am until 2.30pm (except Thursdays) and from 6.30pm in the evening. Sunday hours are from noon until 2.30pm and then from 7 until 10.30pm in the evening.

Flintham

Flintham is an attractive rural community; the layout of Main Street has altered little over the centuries. The arrangement of the cottages along little side lanes off Main Street is particularly pleasing to the eye.

The Walk

If arriving by bus from Nottingham, ask the driver to set you down at Flintham Lane End. Continue walking 100 metres along the A46. Cross over the A46 exercising caution, and turn down the road signposted Flintham to the right. A pleasant half mile walk brings you into the village of Flintham. Bear left with the road, ignoring the turning to the right, and walk along the village main street. Walk past the Boot and Shoe Inn on your left.

(1) Continue past the Boot and Shoe as far as Woods Lane, which lies 50 metres further on the left. Turn down Woods Lane and keep with it as the road becomes a bridleway. You may see gliders overhead from the nearby airfield; these may accompany you throughout the walk. Walk past Hill Farm to your right; this is mainly a collection of renovated buildings.

(2) Walk along the path keeping to the left side of the field. The path then continues straight ahead, and now lies in the middle of two fields. At the end of the field pass through the hedge and turn right, before turning immediately left to continue in a Northwards direction. Carry straight on with the path, which turns into a small road, as you encounter the first houses of Syerston, a small and very attractive village.

(3) Bear left with the road and approach a small green and a junction. Turn right here, noting the church to your left. Continue along this road for 100 yards, taking the footpath signposted to the left, just past a phone box on the right side of the road.

(4) This footpath is marked also by a yellow waymarker, and a diverted footpath sign. Walk along the grassy path to the left of the farm field, over which the footpath used to run. Look to the field on your left, as there may be beehives at the end of the field; each beehive may contain many thousands of bees. Cross over the small brook and bear right with the path. The path continues along the right-hand side of a field. The path bears rightwards around a big tree. Now take the path diagonally across the field to your left; this path is well trodden so any crop should not prove an obstacle. Make for a small group of trees. When you reach the clump of trees, you will find a wooden footpath sign showing that the footpath bears left on the right-hand side of the trees. Follow the

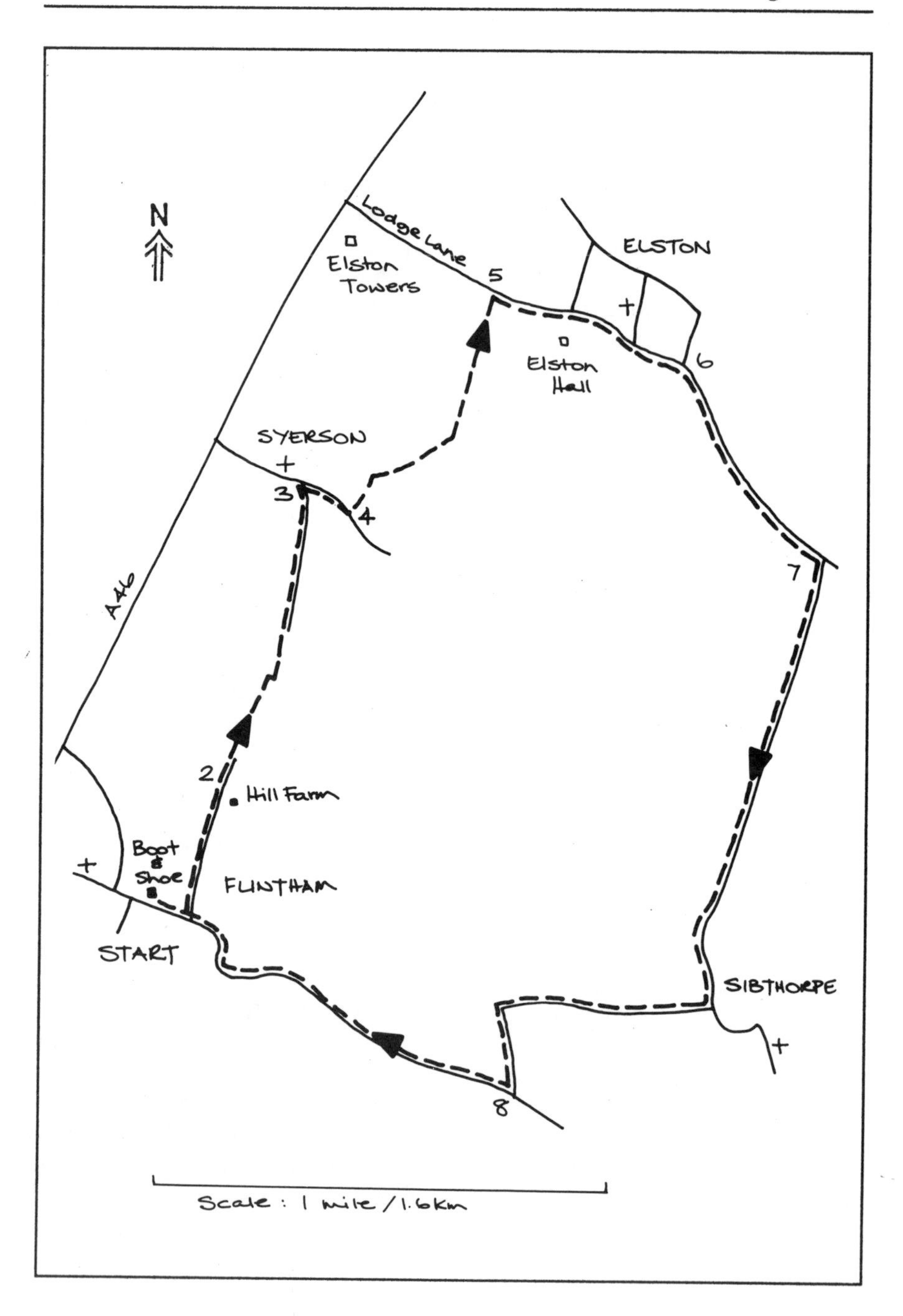
N
Lodge Lane
Elston Towers
5
ELSTON
Elston Hall
6
SYERSON
3
4
A46
7
2
Hill Farm
Boot & Shoe
FLINTHAM
START
SIBTHORPE
8
Scale: 1 mile/1.6km

path along the left-hand edge of the field. The path now crosses into a further field, and lies at the right edge of this field, with a hedge directly to your right. Note Elston Towers to your left; a very curious 19th Century building, described by Pevsner as "really one huge folly". The history of this house is chequered; it was once used as a maggot breeding factory.

(5) Pass through the metal gate at the end of the field, and turn right along Lodge Lane towards the village of Elston. The road bears to the left around Elston Hall, which was owned by the Darwin family between 1680 and 1954. Erasmus Darwin, the grandfather of Charles Darwin, was born here. The Ann Darwin Cottages further along on the right are the results of a bequest in 1772 to provide almshouses. Pass by the attractive Elston Village Stores and Post Office to your left, and notice the modern wishing well in the garden to your right. You will find the Chequers Inn to your left in Toad Lane. This attractive, and recently renovated public house, serves reasonably priced meals at lunchtimes and evenings, also purveying highly drinkable real ale from Wards and Vaux.

(6) After leaving the Chequers, continue along the Main Road, having retraced your steps along Toad Lane, and follow the road out of Elston. The windmill on your right is now restored as a private house, sadly without its sails, but was described by Mee in 1930 as "a windmill like a black giant [which] still grinds the corn".

(7) After half a mile turn right along the road signposted to Sibthorpe/Flintham. Continue along this quiet country lane as it meanders through the bucolic countryside of West Nottinghamshire. A variety of vegetable crops are in the fields here. On entering the village of Sibthorpe, turn right along the lane signposted Flintham, unless you wish to explore Sibthorpe, where a particularly fine dovecote can be viewed. The turning to Flintham has Forge House on the right. Follow this lane; at one point it describes a 90 degree turn to the left.

(8) Turn right at the junction signposted Flintham/Newark, and make your way back to the Boot and Shoe in Flintham, and a well deserved pint of Home Ales.

If you are making your way back to Nottingham by bus, retrace your steps to the main A46, and turn left where you will find the bus stop 100 metres further along the road.

13. LOWDHAM

Route: Lowdham – The Old Hall – Ploughman Wood – Woodborough – Fox Covert – Epperstone – Wash Bridge – Lowdham

Distance: 7 miles

Map: O.S. Pathfinder 813 (Carlton and Elston)

Start: The Magna Charta, Southwell Road, Lowdham

Access: Travel on the A612 road to Lowdham. There is limited on street parking in the village. (Grid Reference 672463). Lowdham is well served by train and bus (Pathfinder and Trent) daily.

The Cross Keys, Epperstone (0602 663033)

The Cross Keys is one of those pubs that make you want to walk this ramble time and time gain. It is a real village pub that has been selected for many years now in the Good Beer Guide and with every good reason. The multi roomed pub is very accommodating and has a separate family room if you have children with you. There are also outdoor patio areas. Hardys and Hansons beers: mild, bitter and Classic are drawn by hand-pump. Home made food is also served at lunch and in the evening until 8.30pm except Sunday evening. The Cross Keys is open from noon until 2.30pm except Mondays and from 6pm each evening. Lunchtime closing is 2.30pm on Sundays, otherwise usual times prevail.

Lowdham

Lowdham is one of Nottingham's larger villages, split in half by a by-pass but nevertheless retaining many quiet corners which add to its charm. The walk passes by two of the village's most interesting houses, The Old Hall has been rebuilt throughout the ages but retains Elizabethan architecture. On the other side of the church is the eccentricity of a house know as The Hut, said to incorporate railway carriages into the upper floors. The area was also known for its corn mills, none of which are still working but several have been converted to dwellings.

Epperstone

Much of the village is now in a conservation area. It is of considerable architectural interest, several houses dating from the 16th century. The church, standing high above the road, is 13th century and nearby are the Manor and well-preserved dovecotes.

The Cross Keys

The Walk

(1) From the Magna Charta turn right to walk up Lowdham's main shopping street with post office, library, take away foods and the like. Pass Tan lane and soon on the right appears the Old School House beautifully restored and with a fine wall clock. Just before the school

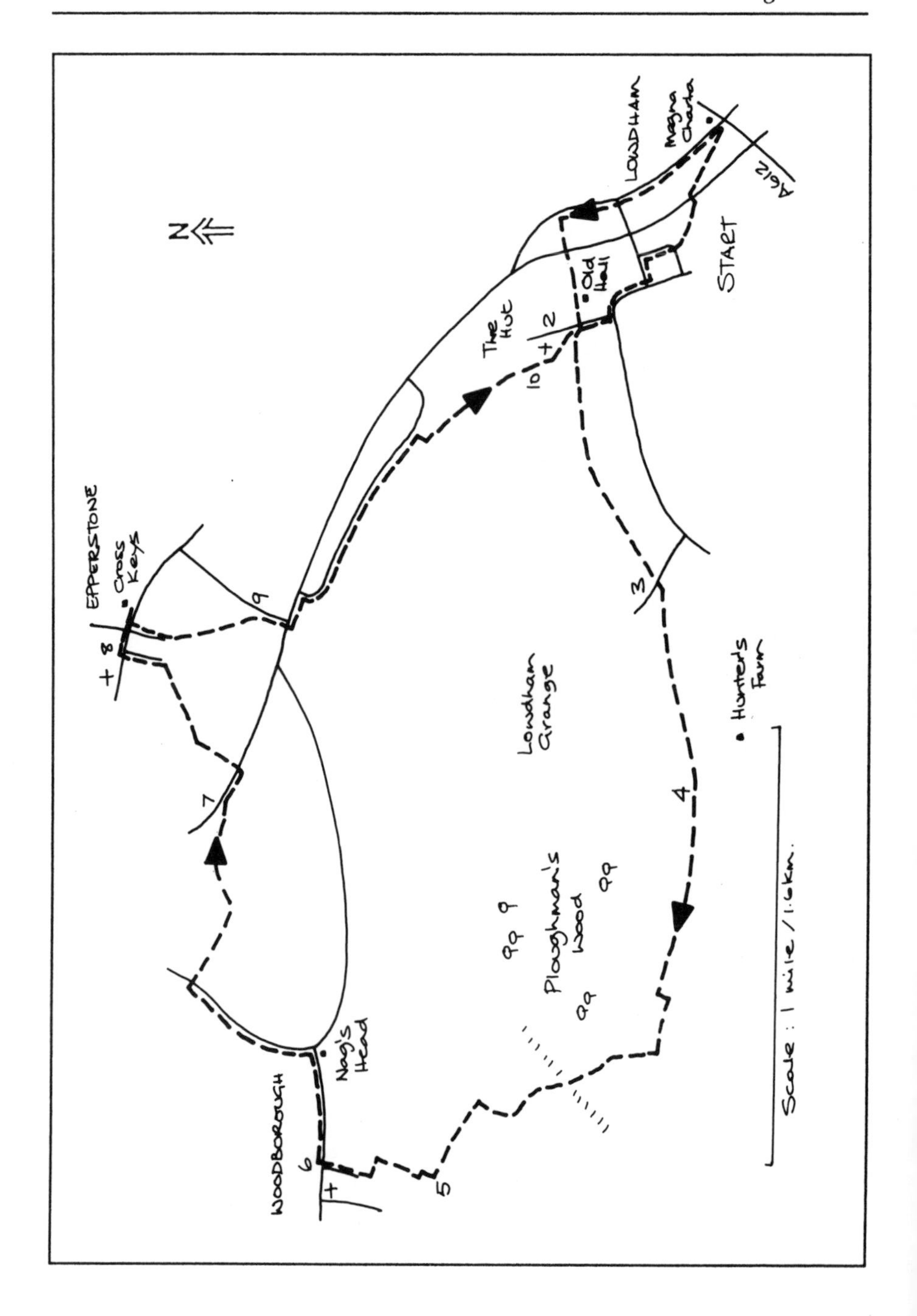
N
LOWDHAM
Magna Charta
A612
START
Old Hall
The Hut
2
10
EPPERSTONE
Cross Keys
9
8
3
Lowdham Grange
Hunters Farm
7
4
Ploughman's Wood
Nag's Head
WOODBOROUGH
6
5
Scale : 1 mile / 1.6km.

grounds turn left along a path signposted to St Mary's church. Cross the main road with care and continue ahead to a lane with The Old Hall to the left. There is a good view across the fields to The Hut, an ornate building of character.

(2) Go right for a few paces then left to enter the churchyard. The path follows the left wall to exit by way of a metal gap stile. The path is here the subject of a diversion. The locals seem to have been using this for some time, so go right up to the field corner and then left along the field's edge. Cross a track and keep ahead with barns at the bottom of the field. Shortly, cross a stile to switch sides of the hedge, still keeping straight on to a road.

(3) Go over the road and stile into a small field. The path bears right to another stile by a white barred gate to the remnants of an old track. Go right and walk up the valley through a succession of fields, the path being clear on the ground and waymarked. To the right stands the austere hillside buildings of Lowdham Grange, once a borstal. The path joins a metalled track but only for 200 paces or so. Hunters Farm stands to your left.

(4) Your way is ahead along a tractor track climbing the gentle valley to eventually reach a stile by white double barred gates. Go ahead through the next field to cross a stile in the boundary hedge opposite with Ploughman Wood to your right. Then go right and through a gap in the next hedge, continuing ahead along the field's edge and by Ploughman wood. The path reaches an edge with a good view of Woodborough below. Go through a gate and bear right to walk along the top edge of the field to a corner but then cut down left to a meeting of tracks. Keep ahead at the gap and keep company with the hedge on the left.

(5) At the corner follow the field's edge down towards the village but look for the path cutting left onto the playing field. Your way is to the right of the field then left along the backs of gardens to a stile. The path then threads its way through allotments and in front of a row of cottages with delightful fronts to the main road. Please pass by with consideration as the path is so near to people's homes.

(6) At the road turn right and pass by many fine red brick buildings that formed the centre of the early framework stocking business of the area.

Turn left at the junction by the Nags Head public house, to leave the village towards fields again. Pass by a house on the right and then almost opposite one on the left cross the road to go down a track to a small building. Go left just before to cross a bridge and the path winds cheerfully alongside a drainage ditch to cross a footbridge at the corner of a wood. Enter another field often in arable crop. The path is shown on the map as heading left across the field to a mid-way point along the left-hand hedge. Locals simply follow the field's edge left and then right to this point where another path from Woodborough is joined. They exit by stile onto the busy road.

(7) Turn right to walk facing the traffic passing the entrance to the old mill on the left. Just beyond is a stile with a curious weathered notice advising walkers that dogs should be on a lead and that Bitches in Season Not Allowed! Cross the stile and keep to the right of the lawn and fence as you make your way from the buildings to a bridge over the old mill leat. The path leads to another concrete bridge and bears right up a track. Cross a stile and head right to skirt the edge of playing fields. The spire of Epperstone church can be seen and the village stands ahead on the rise.

Cross a stile and go right between two tall beech trees to a gap stile by a gate. Walk ahead along a track to join Bland lane. Turn left and follow this to a junction opposite a large sandstone wall. A diversion to the church on the left is worthwhile.

(8) Otherwise, turn right to walk along the main street to the Cross Keys public house. From the pub walk back towards the church but at the crossroads go left down a narrow lane. At the bottom corner, keep ahead to walk along a path between house and cottage into fields. Cross a stile into a large field and head diagonally left to the top far left corner where a footbridge is crossed.

(9) Meet a road and turn right to walk over the footbridge to the main road. Cross the main road to the left of a garage to join the much quieter old Epperstone Road. Pass by houses and then a nursery on the right. The road begins to bend left with a row of houses on the left. Here, go right through a gap and follow the field track through a small enclosure. Once through the next gap go left to climb up the bank of the field to a high point above Lowdham. By a straggly and solitary tree, keep ahead

towards the church spire. The Hut is to the left and in the distance, the cliff above the Trent and a windmill on Kneeton Road beyond.

(10) The path drops down by the churchyard to the point where you started. On reaching the lane by Old Hall do not go left, however, but keep ahead up to a main road. Go left and follow this around to Tan Lane. Go right into Plough lane to pass The Worlds End pub. At the corner beyond, go left along the fields edge away from the drive on the left. Pass by a small orchard to meet another path coming down from the hillside. Go left to the main road. Cross over and walk a few paces to the right. Go left through the gap into the playing fields and green. Head right across the fields to Main St and the Magna Charta.

14. LOWDHAM TO THURGARTON

Route: Lowdham Railway station – Hoveringham Mill – Gonalston Road – Thurgarton Railway Station and village

Distance: 3 miles

Map: O.S. Pathfinder 813 Carlton and Elston

Access: Lowdham is on the A612 road and there is limited on street parking on Station Road. A far better bet is to use the train for this rail ramble or the Pathfinder bus. This is a linear walk, so use the train or bus to return to the starting point. There is a regular daily service between the two villages.

The Red Lion, Thurgarton (0636 830351)

The Red Lion stands by the roadside in Thurgarton, not much more of a stone's throw away from the Coach and Horses. This well appointed establishment offers a welcome to ramblers. A macabre tale is told in newspaper cuttings, framed and illustrated on the walls, about the murder of a previous landlady. She was killed by her niece on August Bank Holiday, 1930, in mysterious circumstances. Food is served at The Red Lion during opening times that are 11.30am until 2.30pm and from 6.30pm in the evening from Mondays to Saturdays. The following beers are available on handpull- Mansfield's Riding Bitter and Old Baily, John Smith's Bitter and Courage Directors.

Thurgarton

The roadside village of Thurgarton elevated from the lower levels of the Trent Valley is a fitting end to this ramble. At the very edge of the village is Thurgarton priory church – a Victorian restoration on the site of an earlier building that became a ruin well before the last century. The original priory was destroyed at the time of the Dissolution but a house still stands on the former grounds. One unusual feature in the village is the clock on the right of the main road. This comes from Nottingham's Midland station, one of the many railway artifacts gathered by the owner of the property which is private.

The Church, Lowdham

The Walk

(1) The walk commences from Lowdham railway station. Cross the tracks in the direction of Gunthorpe and then turn next left to walk along the Caythorpe Road. Pass by the Old Volunteer pub and then on the next straight section go left through a gateway, opposite the Cricket and Hockey Club sign, into a the large field.

(2) Follow the clear track, which happens to be a bridleway, as it curves gently to the right towards the buildings of Hoveringham mill which date from the last years of the 18th century. Go through the gates and then cross a bridge by the ford at the mill, a splendid building with red roses adorning the warm red bricks of this classic mill complex that evidently worked until the early 1960s.

(3) Walk along the drive away from the mill, but look for a small gate on the left to enter a field. Go left along the hedgerow and then right, as signposted along the field's edge by the clear water of a drainage ditch. Cross the Hoveringham road with Gonalston crossing to the left and beyond a glimpse of Gonalston church.

(4) The walk proceeds ahead, still following the water channel until it approaches the aggregate extraction, a large hole in the ground festooned with keep out notices. Sound advice. Go left and left again over two footbridges now following the left-hand side of the channel through thicker undergrowth. The path turns right before the railway and wanders between it and the channel until finally giving out onto a track used by quarry vehicles.

(5) Exit onto the main road and turn left for the station, the platform on this south side being for trains to Lowdham and Nottingham. Cross the tracks for Thurgarton village. Cross to the other side of the road and on the corner a well worn path leads off diagonally across the field towards the village. It exits at the corner of a road. Walk around the corner and ahead to the main road opposite the entrance to Thurgarton priory. Turn right for the village centre and The Red Lion public house. Suitably refreshed, return to the station for a train or catch the Pathfinder bus back from the village.

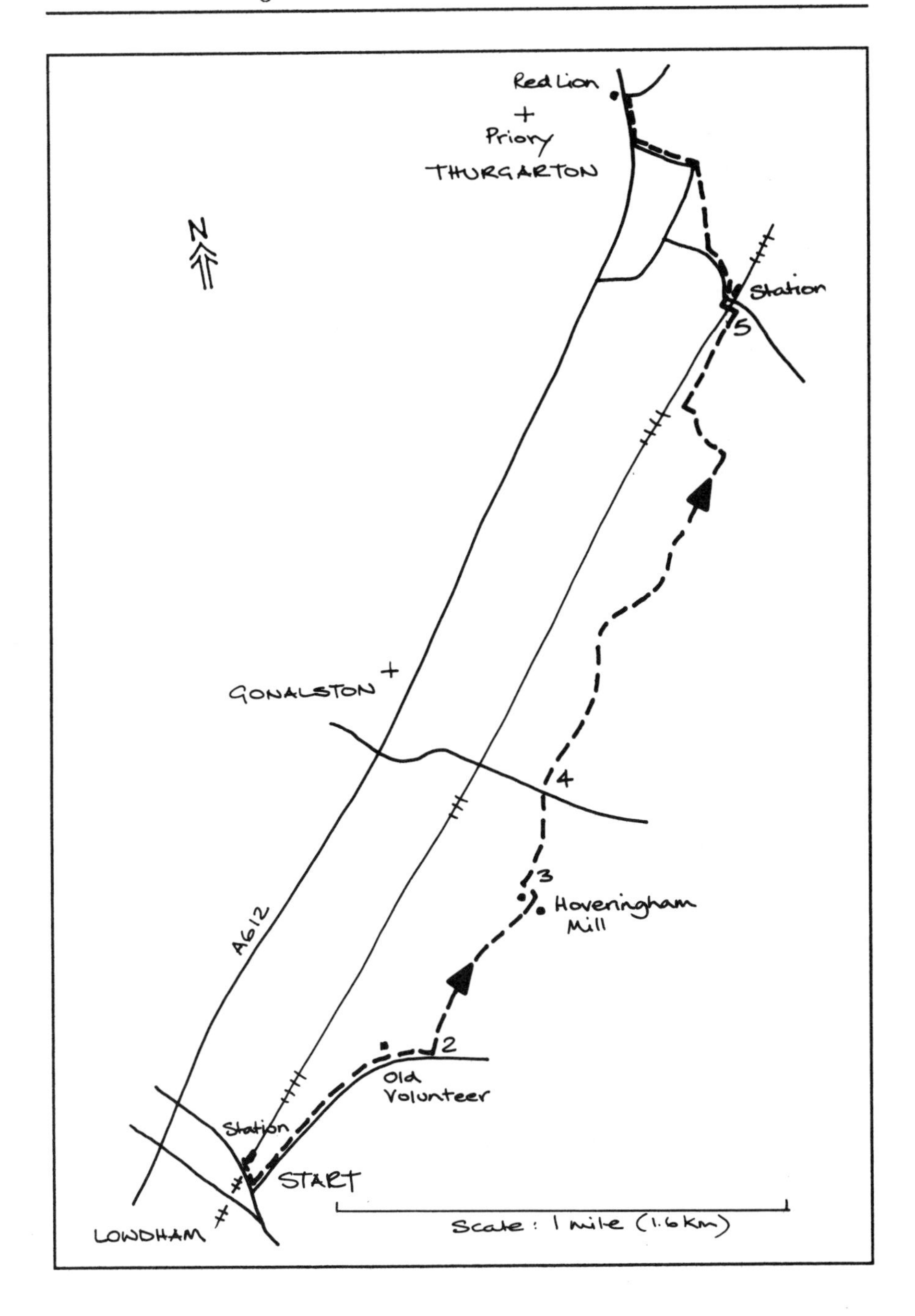
Red Lion
Priory
THURGARTON
N
Station
5
GONALSTON
4
3
Hoveringham
Mill
A612
2
Old
Volunteer
Station
START
LOWDHAM
Scale: 1 mile (1.6km)

15. BAGTHORPE

Route: Shepherd's Rest – Underwood Hill – Wansley Hall – Bagthorpe Brook – Home Farm – Lea Road (Selston Common) – Inkerman – Shepherd's Rest.

Distance: 3 miles

Map: O.S. Pathfinder 795 Sutton in Ashfield

Start: Roadside Parking at Wansley Hall (Grid Reference SK 462514)

Access: Daily bus services to Selston Common. Bus-stop at Lea Road end. Travel by car on the M1 to the junction with A608. Follow the A608 to Underwood then right to Underwood Hill. Turn right again at Wansley Hall crossroads, signposted Bagthorpe.

The Shepherd's Rest, Lower Bagthorpe (0773 810506)

The Shepherd's Rest at Lower Bagthorpe is a lovely pub serving draught Mild and Bitter Home Ales beers. It has two bars, and the public bar is ideal for walkers. A lively pub, with a fine collection of plates commemorating the various local collieries, miners' union branches etc. Food is served daily and there is a children's play area outside and a large beer garden with seats and tables. In summer the pub is renowned for its barbecues and annual duck race on August Bank Holiday Monday. Opening hours are Mondays to Fridays 12 noon until 3pm, 6pm opening in the evenings; Saturday all day from noon, but in the winter, hours are more restricted. Usual Sunday hours prevail.

Bagthorpe

The hamlet of Bagthorpe lies between the two larger Erewash valley villages of Underwood and Snelston. The area has seen the continuous development of mining throughout the centuries until recent decades. During the intense period of industrialisation during the last century several of these villages also witnessed an increase in framework knitting and ironstone extraction.

The Shepherd's Rest

The Walk

(1) From Wansley Hall walk down the hill to the footpath signs and take the route on the left. Go over the stile and into fields. The path is wet underfoot, but distinct, keeping alongside the left-hand hedge. Despite being a rural area there is an ever present dull rumbling noise, the traffic on the M1, over a mile away. A second stile takes you into another wet field and the path descends to a clump of bushes in the bottom left-hand corner. Here again there is a stile and a path leads off to the left. Ignore this and continue down, through the bushes to the bridge spanning the Bagthorpe Brook.

(2) Across the bridge go through a rough field with the hedge on your right to reach another stile. Bear right, diagonally across the field to a stile and bridge. Beyond the bridge the path forks. Your route lies to the right, following the stream which is well disguised with a thick covering of hawthorn and other bushes. Part way along the field there is a path leading off left to an obvious stile. Ignore this and continue beside the

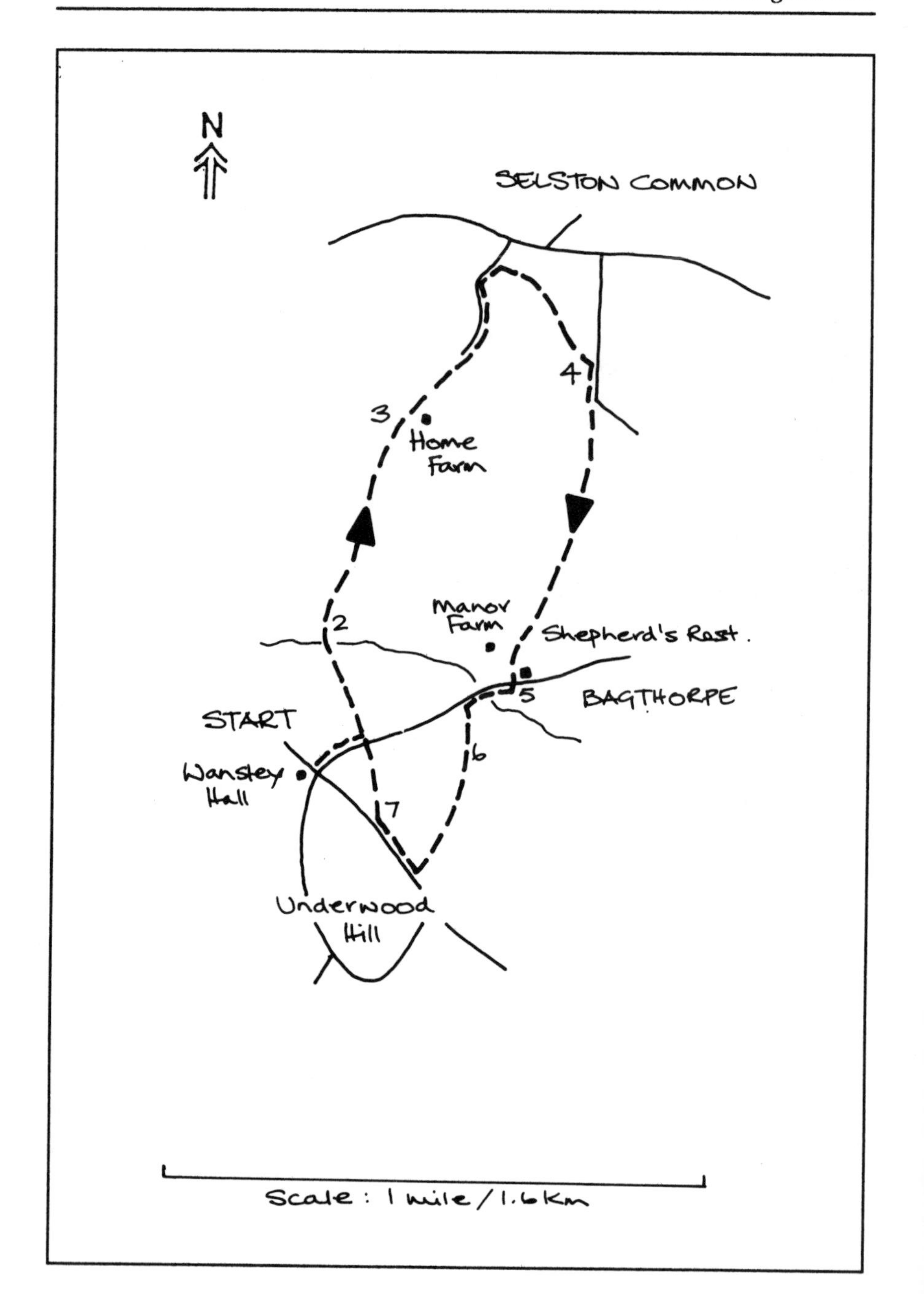
N
SELSTON COMMON
4
3
Home Farm
2
Manor Farm
Shepherd's Rest.
5
BAGTHORPE
START
6
Wansley Hall
7
Underwood Hill
Scale: 1 mile/1.6Km

stream to a gateway. This hides the fact that the stream is culverted at this point, so once through the gate you will find the stream on your left. Continue up the broad track with the new conifer plantation on your right to reach a step stile by a gate. The buildings of Home Farm are on your right.

(3) Go over the stile and proceed alongside the buildings. Another step stile takes you out onto the access to the farm. Ignoring the waymarked stile on the left, continue along the farm access which soon reaches the first houses of Selston and leads into Lea Lane. Here, go right and proceed past the playing field on the left, until you almost reach the main road. Then on the right there is a narrow driveway which is signed as leading to certain houses on Nottingham Road. (Public transport users will join the walk at this point. There is a bus stop at the top of Lea Lane. Go down Lea Lane for a short way, then on the left is the narrow driveway mentioned above.) Go down this track and continue straight ahead, closely hemmed in by houses and bungalows on either side, until another road is crossed. The track continues ahead, signed with a "No Cycling" notice. This part of the path is even more closely confined by fences and hedges, but it is tarred and presents no difficulties. The path crosses a small stream by a bridge and then rises through the fields of Allens Green, though still fenced either side. The path eventually emerges on a road opposite a very derelict shop.

(4) This area is named on the map as Inkerman. It is one of several place names in the area derived from the Crimean War of the 1850s.

Go right at the road, passing a side turning on the left and Melbourne House Farm on the right and continuing until the telephone box is reached. Here the road goes left to Alma, another Crimean War name, but your route lies ahead, over the stile to the right of the telephone box. Keeping the hedge to the left, proceed down through a couple of fields passing underneath the electricity wires to reach two stiles. Ignore the one on the left and go through the other, which is waymarked and heads towards Manor Farm. Just before the farm is reached, there is another stile and this leads into a narrow fenced and hedged path. A gap in the left-hand hedge gives direct access to the Shepherd's Rest pub.

(5) Leaving the pub, go right, along the road and cross the bridge over the Bagthorpe Brook. Just beyond the bridge there is a footpath sign on

the right. Ignore this, but look on the opposite side of the road for a stile. Do not go through the tempting gate, but negotiate the stile and follow the hedge up the field. At the next stile, all evidence of a path on the ground ceases.

(6) The route shown on the OS map should lie in a straight line towards the pylon, but there is a fence in the way. There is a gateway in the fence to the right of the pylon or alternatively, if you follow the left-hand edge of the field, by the stream, there is a stile of sorts. If you follow the latter route you should then head up the next field to a stile in the top hedge, close to the left-hand corner. The stile is marked with a sign post and lies to the left of a wooden electricity pylon. On reaching this stile go over it into the road at Underwood Hill and turn right. In less than 100 metres there is another signpost and stile on the right. To your consternation you will realise that this takes you back into the field you have just left! Bear left once in the field again, to reach a stile in the opposite hedge, less than 50 metres down the field.

The significance of the gateway mentioned previously now becomes apparent. By using this and following up the right-hand side of the field instead of the left, you will reach this stile without having to scale three other stiles and without any road walking. There is some evidence on the ground that this is done by local walkers, though strictly speaking you are not on the right of way.

(7) Go through the exit stile and extricate yourself from the quagmire on the other side. The path skirts the right-hand end of the farm building and fence to another stile, then runs alongside a hedge on the left. The finely restored buildings of Wansley Hall are on the left, and, as these are reached, there is a further stile. A quick sprint across the last little paddock takes you to the final stile and the road where the walk began.

16. ROLLESTON

Route: Rolleston – Upton – Upton Mill – Southwell Racecourse – Rolleston

Distance: 4 miles

Map: O.S. Pathfinder 796 (Newark-on-Trent West)

Start: Rolleston church (Grid Reference 742526)

Access: Travel on the Fiskerton road from Southwell (turning at Easthorpe) turning left before Fiskerton railway station. Turn left at Averham for Rolleston if approaching from Newark. There is limited parking in Rolleston. There is a daily train service from Nottingham and Newark to Rolleston (5 minutes walk from the church) and a Mondays to Saturdays bus link from Newark and Southwell.

The Crown, Rolleston (0636 814358)

The Crown public house, dating from the 1830s and in the centre of Rolleston, welcomes the rambler to this homely establishment. It is known to many racegoers, as it is the nearest hostelry to Southwell races. It is also known to older people as there used to be a large tree which had an opening in its trunk through which newly weds walked in the hope of the custom bringing good luck. Marstons Pedigree is on handpull and food is served at all times. Families are welcome and there is a garden to the rear. The Crown is open from 11am until 3pm and from 6.30pm in the evenings except Saturday when evening opening begins at 6 pm.

The Cross Keys, Upton (0636 813269)

The Cross Keys at Upton is a compulsory stop on this ramble! This old coaching inn dating from the 17th century is full of character with a bar, lounge and restaurant in a former dovecote. Not surprisingly, the Cross keys has an exceptional reputation for good food and beer. On handpull are Boddingtons Bitter, Brakspears Bitter, Marstons Pedigree, Bateman's

XXXB and regular guest beers. The pub is said to be haunted by a cloaked figure with a wide-brimmed hat, an apparition evidently witnessed in another old building a few doors away. The hosts experienced many unusual happenings when they first moved in during 1984 such as taps being turned on and off but nothing of a malicious nature.

Rolleston

Home to the famous creator of child pictures, Kate Greenaway, whose drawings were used to illustrate Christmas cards and poetry throughout Europe, Rolleston is a quiet backwater. The church dates from the 12th century and contains many interesting artefacts including an original paper register written by the then vicar Robert Leband at the turn of the 17th century who unfortunately drowned in one of the many water ditches in the parish.

Upton

Surrounding the beautiful church dating from medieval times and with a 15th century tower the village of Upton is now mainly in a conservation area with many distinctive red brick buildings with pantile roofs along the main road. Pity about the traffic! The village has, however, stood the test of time, for Upton Hall is the home of the British Horological Institute, which is open occasionally to visitors.

The Walk

(1) Turn right from Rolleston church to the road junction and then bear left to walk by houses and The Crown public house. Continue on the left-hand side of the road to the end of the village where there is a green track between houses leading to the railway. Cross with great care then bear slightly right across a field to a footbridge. Go over this and head slightly right again across the next field to join a wider track.

(2) Go through a gap, turn right and then left now proceeding along the field's edge in this very flat flood plain landscape so far dominated by arable cropping. Cross a footbridge and a stile to enter what is now a

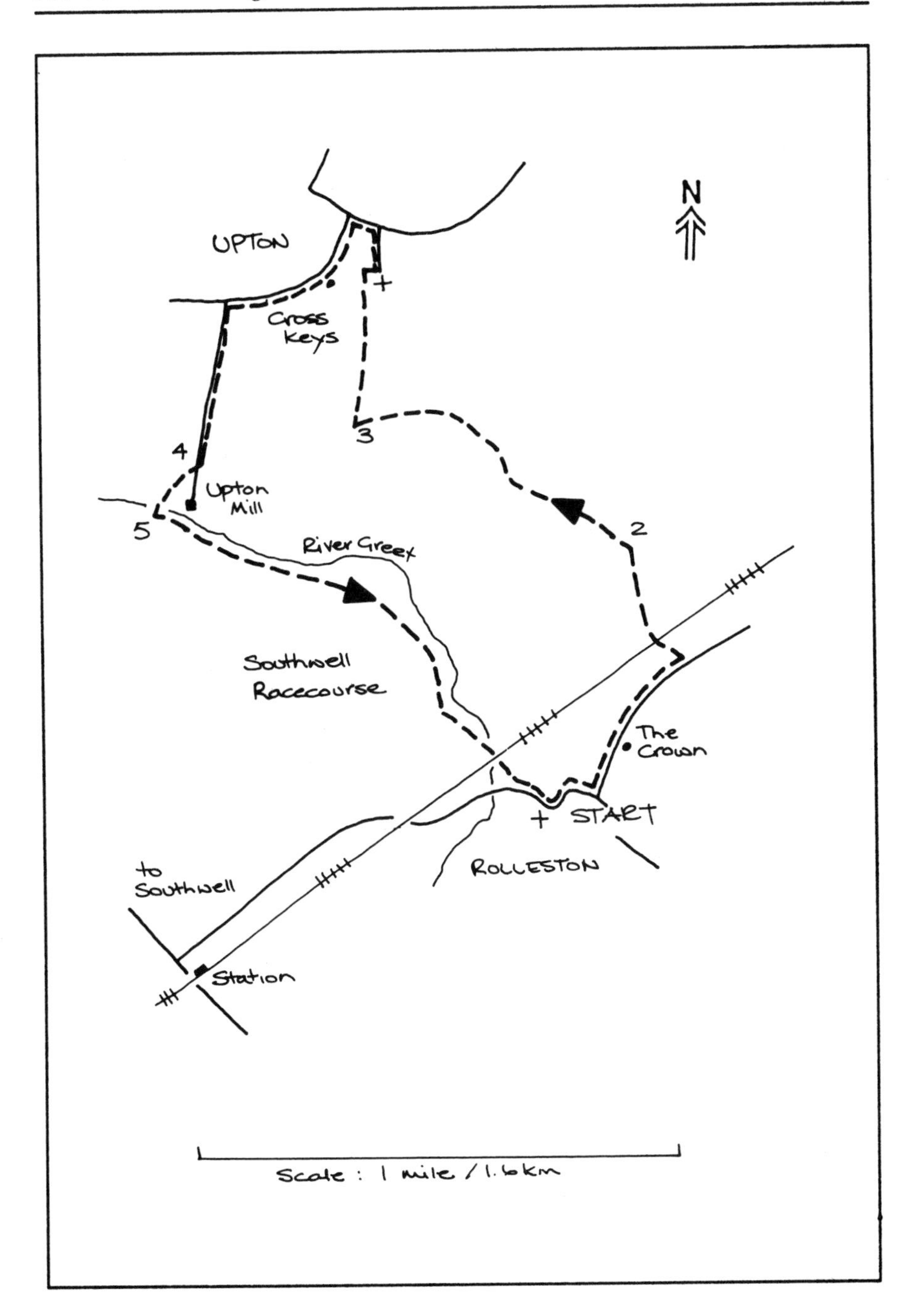
N
UPTON
Cross Keys
3
4
Upton Mill
5
2
River Greet
Southwell Racecourse
The Crown
START
ROLLESTON
to Southwell
Station
Scale : 1 mile / 1.6km

grazing pasture, once a local centre for the growing of flax. Walk ahead to join a fence by a ditch. Follow this to another stile onto a track. Go right and immediately left, now following a larger water channel on the left. Go ahead to cross another stile that brings you to a green lane.

(3) Walk along the lane but look for a stile on the right. Cross this and keep company with the hedge to a tractor bridge. Cross this and walk up the bank to Upton church, the path being a section of the Trent Valley Way. At the churchyard go right and then left in Church lane to reach the main road. Turn left and walk along the pavement through this lovely village, passing by the entrance to the British Horological Institute dating from 1858. Next is The Cross keys, which is an essential visit. You will also pass a Wesleyan Chapel dating from 1831 and opposite the old school turn left down a lane for Upton Mill.

(4) As you approach the mill, the lane goes over a bridge. Cross a stile on the right and head diagonally across the field to the far left corner. Cross the double stile and follow the River Greet up to the bridge which is crossed.

(5) Once over turn left and follow the field boundary around the back of the mill complex. Then continue over a stile by a gate and ahead onto grazing land. The path keeps to the left of Southwell racecourse and to the right of the embankment of the River Greet. It curves right as the river does, crosses a stile in a fence and heads towards a track, the river and mill standing to the left in the near distance. Join the track and walk by the mill to the railway line. Cross the tracks and go to a road. Turn right for Rolleston railway station and left for the church.

17. SOUTHWELL

Route: Southwell Minster – Brackenhurst – Cundy Hill – Westhorpe – Southwell Minster

Distance: 3.5 miles

Map: O.S. Pathfinder 796 (Newark-on-Trent West)

Start: Southwell Minster (Grid Reference 703537)

Access: Southwell is on the A612 from Averham near Newark and from Nottingham. There is car parking in Church Street. The town enjoys an excellent service from Nottingham and Newark by Pathfinder buses daily. Other companies also offer a service between Newark and Southwell.

The Hearty Goodfellow (0636 812365)

This pleasant pub on Church Street takes its name from a well known Victorian balled which appears on the pub wall:

"I am a hearty goodfellow
I live at my ease
I work when I am ready
I play when I please
With my bottle and glass
Many hours do I pass
Sometimes with a friend
Sometimes with a lass. "

The pub has a friendly atmosphere and offers two unusual beers on handpull, Everards Old Original and Adnams Southwold bitter. Food is served from noon until 2pm and Friday, Saturday and Sunday nights from 7pm until 10 pm. Families can only be accommodated when eating, but there is a large and well kept garden to the rear of the house. The Hearty Goodfellow is open from 11am until 2pm and from 6pm in the evenings on Mondays to Saturdays. Usual Sunday opening hours. The authors also recommend the nearby Bramley Apple, another recent entry to The Good Beer Guide.

Southwell

Southwell Minster is one of the loveliest buildings in the land. It has many exceptional pieces of architecture including a 13th century Chapter House and carved stone screen. Its location in the centre of this small Georgian and Victorian centre heightens the appeal to the visitor and the ramble offers several excellent views over the town. Southwell is a bustling centre, partly because of the schools and partly by retaining its function as a local shopping centre. Among local notables was Lord Byron who resided here for a few years having moved from Newstead Abbey which was falling about his head. Southwell is where the Bramley Apple evolved, a really good cooking apple that can be bought in the shops hereabouts. Orcharding still exists in the area as a commercial activity as well as the many gardens that feature a variety of fruit trees in this sheltered part of the county.

The Walk

(1) From the Minster grounds walk down Church street towards Easthorpe and just before the Hearty Goodfellow, over the bridge, go right along a narrow path alongside the Potwell Dyke. This passes by a school on the right. Keep ahead by the playing fields and then head right and left to exit onto a lane by sports pavilions and tennis courts. Go left and by the end building bear right off the road to a footbridge. Then head up the path between a broken fence and hedge. This can get very overgrown so locals usually skirt the edge of the playing fields to a the corner.

(2) Go through the gap to enter a field and walk up the bank keeping company with the hedge to your left. This well beaten path rises to the top of the field where you go right to a gateway leading into the next field. Take a look back over Southwell, the fine building of the minster rising above the surrounding the central cluster of houses and shops. Head left across the field to exit at a gateway just to the left of the top right corner. You will see a signpost when closer.

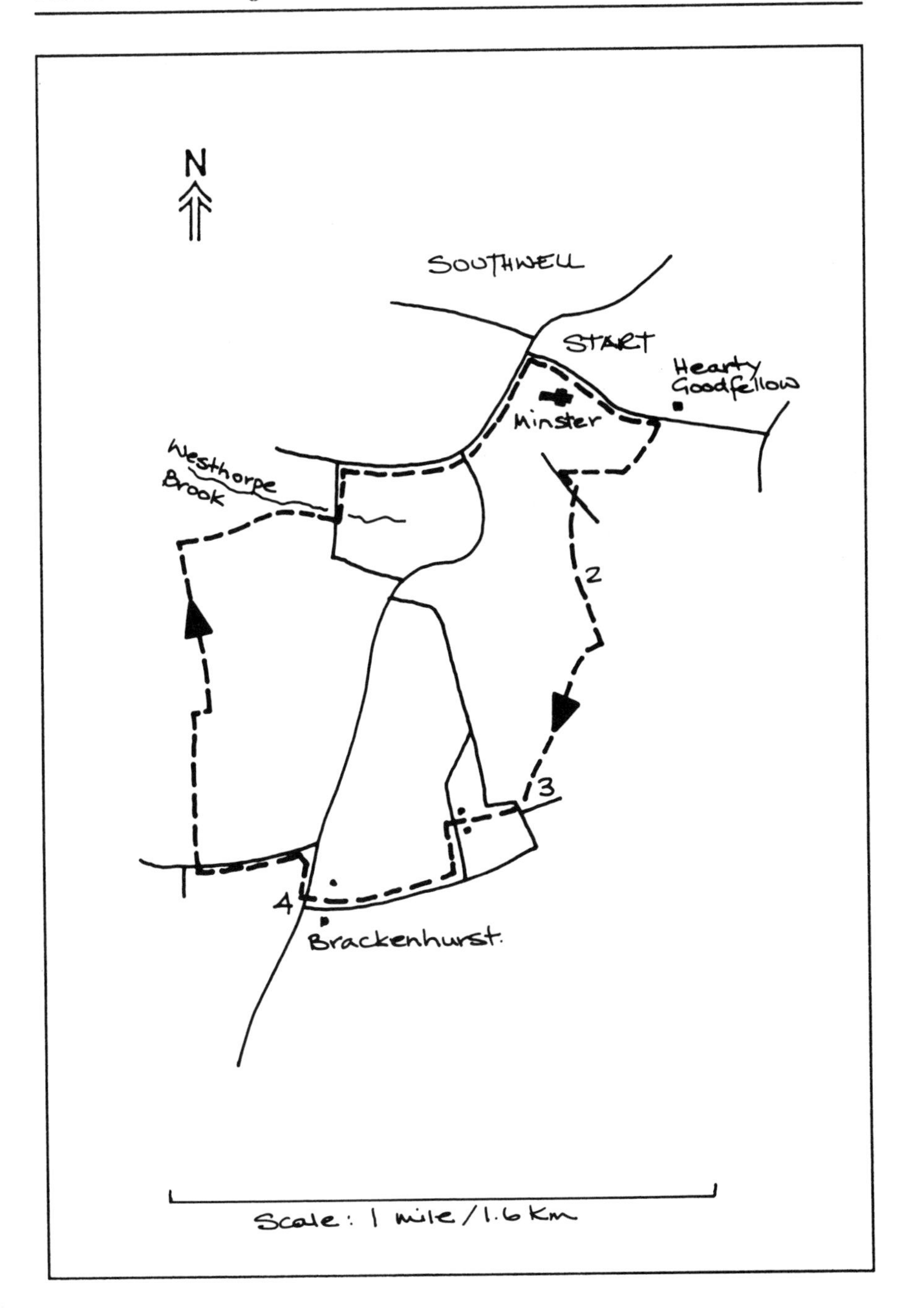
N
SOUTHWELL
START
Hearty Goodfellow
Minster
Westhorpe Brook
2
3
4
Brackenhurst
Scale: 1 mile/1.6 Km

(3) Turn right on the road but at the corner beyond the cottage keep ahead as signposted. This little path is part of the Brackenhurst Farm trail and there are information boards explaining the farming practices being practised at this college of agriculture. At the next road go left, then right at the crossroads. Pass by the main college buildings including the hall itself on the left which was originally built in the 1820s for the vicar of Halloughton

(4) At the main road go right but cross to walk through the picnic area to then turn left along a lane. Shortly, go right through a gate and keep ahead with a hedge to your left to Cundy Hill offering good views of Southwell. Go through another gate and walk down the field to the corner, right and then next left as signposted. Proceed through the gap ahead and descend the hill to a lush corner by Westhorpe brook. Another path is joined here and this dips down into the dumble. You, however, keep ahead to follow the field's edge around to a stile. The well-worn path then follows the stream between garden tippings and the like to a road. Turn left and climb the bank to the main road. Turn right for the Minster.

18. KIRKBY IN ASHFIELD

Route: Kirkby in Ashfield – Boar Hill – Shire Carr – Pinxton Lane – Crow Trees Farm – The Dumbles – Kirkby in Ashfield

Distance: 4 miles

Map: O.S. Pathfinder 795 Sutton in Ashfield

Start: The Duke of Wellington, Kirkby in Ashfield (Grid Reference SK 490562)

Access: There is a frequent daily bus service from Mansfield and Nottingham. A train service is proposed! Travel on the A38 from M1 or Mansfield, to junction with B6018, then follow signs to Kirkby. The Duke of Wellington is just beyond the mini roundabout. There is ample roadside parking.

The Duke of Wellington, Kirkby in Ashfield

The Duke of Wellington is, according to the landlord, a spooky place. The ghosts are of a friendly nature and on Halloween regular ghost spotters are known to hold an all night vigil here – a good excuse if ever there was one! The pub serves Mansfield Riding bitter and Old Baily. It is open all day throughout the week and usual Sunday hours. Families are welcome and there are benches in the garden. Food is served lunchtimes and evenings except on Saturday and Sunday evenings.

Kirkby in Ashfield

This traditional Nottinghamshire mining community grew from the smallest hamlets in the last century to a considerable sized centre. Kirkby now serves mainly as a dormitory town for Mansfield and Nottingham.

The Walk

(1) From the pub go across the road and up the driveway. In a very short distance there is a narrow enclosed path on the left, running along the right-hand side of St. Wilfred's parish hall. The path is walled on the left and there is a fence to the right. Another driveway is crossed at the head of a cul de sac, then the narrow path resumes until it finally emerges into open fields. Here go right and follow the hedge and fence, ignoring the driveway into Eyefield and the two stiles leading into the playing fields.

(2) At the second stile on the right, the path leaves the shelter of the hedge and bears left, making a bee line for the gateway that can be seen ahead. This manoeuvre is likely to involve going through whatever crops there are in the field and there is some evidence that walkers go round the edge of the field to reach the gateway. However, the direct route is the right of way.

(3) At the gateway, the map shows a path going straight ahead and another turning left. The path ahead is clear enough, again clipping the corner of the field to reach a kink in the boundary hedge. Of the other path there is no sign and this is most unfortunate, for this is your route. When this walk was reconnoitred, the field was ploughed and there was no sign of anyone having attempted the right of way line. Many had followed the other path though and this quickly leads to a wide track which turns left and begins to descend the field, keeping to the foot of the unploughed bank. The track hugs the bottom of the bank and turns right. At this point you are not far off the correct line of the path. The bank now begins to level out and where it finishes, the track swings to the left, heading down towards Franderground Farm. Where the track turns left, the path should go straight on, but it doesn't, so follow the track to the bottom of the field and there go right, alongside the hedge and ditch. In a short distance there is a stile on the left and a slippery plank bridge over the ditch. Go left here, over the plank and the stile, into another field.

(4) In this field the path is again not immediately obvious, but the route lies across to the gateway in the middle of the opposite hedge, heading for the group of pylons. The final stretch to the gateway is very wet after

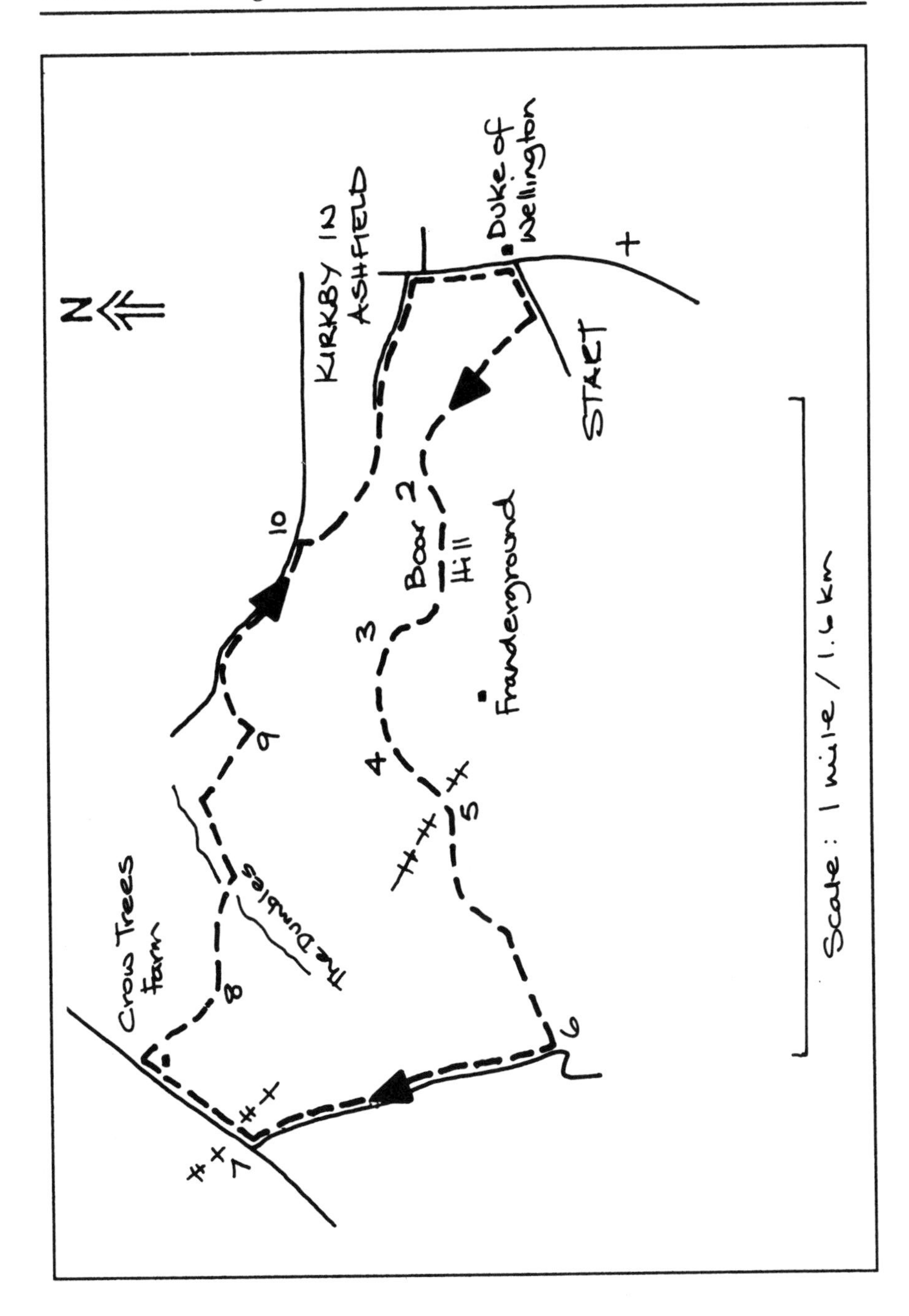
N
KIRKBY IN ASHFIELD
Duke of Wellington
START
Boar Hill
Crow Trees Farm
The Dumbles
1
2
3
4
5
6
7
8
9
10
Scale: 1 mile / 1.6 km

heavy rain and your boots will feel as if they have been lined with lead. Go through the way-marked gate and ignoring the track running by the right-hand hedge, bear left across the field, heading to the right of the first wooden pylon. Although this path crosses the middle of the field it is obvious underfoot and leads unerringly to a gate in the opposite hedge. Here the path is supposed to fork, but this is not obvious on the ground, so keep left, by the hedge to reach a stile on the right of a gate.

(5) The stile and gate guarded a crossing over the former Great Central Railway. This was one of the last main lines to be built in this country, only being constructed in the closing years of the 19th century. It was destined to have a short life by railway standards, falling victim to a combination of railway politics and dubious economics in the late 1960s. Cross the railway to another stile and there bear right towards the third pylon on the skyline. When the field boundary is reached, there is a stile, though it is scarcely of any relevance. Go through, round or over the stile depending on inclination and head straight across the next field, to the left of the pylon seen earlier, towards the right-hand end of a line of bushes. The map shows a field boundary to be negotiated, but it doesn't exist. So, when the line of bushes is reached, turn right and follow this tatty remnant of a hedge until it reaches a gateway into a narrow track.

(6) Turn right at the track and then shortly bear left, through the waymarked bridlegate. This is an excellent spot for observing the slow moving traffic on the nearby M1. It would also have been a good spot for watching the trains go by on the Great Central main line. The bridleway, closely hedged throughout, dips to reach the stream that passes through the delightful little woodland called The Dumbles. Here there is a substantial bridge, which is crossed and the track then ascends the far bank. Keeping the hedge on your left until the corner, climb the field, then head straight for the gate and stile that brings you out onto Pinxton Lane.

(7) At the road go right, towards Crow Trees Farm. You pass over the site of the former Great Central Railway line, now completely removed, the bridge demolished and the cutting filled in. As you approach Crow Trees Farm, the tip of the steeple of Kirkby in Ashfield church is seen to the right. Just beyond the farm, there is a waymarked path to the right. Go down this path, which doubles as the driveway to the farm, and, keeping close to the hedge on the left, leave the buildings behind. There

is an extensive view to the right, over the M1 towards Pinxton. The forlorn truncated remains of the railway embankment can be seen, now completely grown over.

(8) The path follows the hedge closely as it bends first to the left and then to the right, descending steadily into the trees that mark The Dumbles. The path crosses the brook by a culvert and then ascends the far bank. Ignore paths going off left and right and continue up until you reach the edge of a field. Here the path forks. Ignore the route over the stile into the field and bear left instead, keeping just inside the wood, with the hedge on your right.

(9) Where the wood ends, the path swings abruptly right, into a narrow, wet, hollow way. This climbs steadily for about 200 metres, closely hemmed in with bushes, then turns sharp left. Still climbing, but not so steeply, the track reaches a junction with the access to Dumbles Bungalow at a set of white gateposts. The enclosing hedge is not so enveloping here and the route is no longer a hollow way, so there is quite a surprisingly wide view, including Crich Stand and Alport Hill.

(10) As the track tops the brow of the hill, the spire of Kirkby church comes into view ahead and to the right At this point the lane bears left. The OS map shows two paths heading off across the fields on the right, and another joining the lane on the left. Look out for a band of yellow plastic on one of the burnt remnants of the hedge on the right. This is the "waymark". It is just before a gateway on the right and opposite the waymarked gateway on the left. However, it takes a brave walker to set off across a field of sugar beet when there's no obvious path. But, if you head for the church spire you will find, to your surprise, that a well-beaten path soon appears. In the centre of the field there is a well defined crossing of paths. Go left here and soon reach the edge of the field. Continue straight on with the hedge on your right, to enter Cow Pasture Lane near Pasture Farm. This soon emerges on the main road, at the roundabout, by the remains of the cross. Go right here, along the main road and thus reach the Duke of Wellington.

19. CAUNTON

Route: Caunton – Winkhill – Maplebeck – Caunton

Distance: 8 miles (farmland and minor roads)

Map: O.S. Pathfinder 780 (Ollerton) and 796 (Newark on Trent)

Start: Caunton bus shelter (opposite church). (Grid reference SK 745600)

Access: Travel Wright 32, Ollerton – Newark. Infrequent service on Sherwood Forester Network. The Retford – Newark bus also passes by. Caunton is just off the A616 road between Newark and Ollerton. Car parking is available in the village.

The Beehive, Maplebeck (0636 86306)

The original pub was just one small room, but it has now expanded to two rooms of this old house. Even so, it is still the smallest pub in the county, and it can only accommodate the number of people that is does by having several tables in the beautifully kept garden. It has genuine charm and good beer: Riding and Old Baily from nearby Mansfield.

Caunton

Caunton is a pleasing village, separated from the busy main road by the imposing grounds of Caunton Manor. This has been the home of the Hole family since the 15th century, including Samuel Reynolds Hole, the founder of the Rose Society. It possesses an outstanding bus shelter, complete with hanging baskets of geraniums, a pleasant pub called The Plough, and it still has a ford. The church of St. Andrew is worth a look.

The Walk

(1) From the bus shelter opposite the church turn right, and take the first road on the right by the hopefully re-opened Hole pub. On your left Caunton Manor can be glimpsed through the gateways with its extensive grounds, and on your right you will see the old ford on Ford Lane. Follow the road as it turns left by the manor wall, with the tennis courts to your right.

At the main road turn right, and after 200 metres cross over and take the side road signposted Maplebeck 2 miles. Follow the road,

Admiring the fine views of Beesthorpe Hall to the right, and after 1200 metres note a wooden footpath sign on the left by the drive to Readyfield Farm. Do not be surprised if a pack of 40 hounds bound across the fenced-in field on your left; they can't get over the wire, so keep calm!

(2) Follow the drive towards the farm and then head off right across the field, aiming for the left-hand corner of Duke's Wood some 300 metres away. At the corner of the wood a yellow waymarker leads you through a gate, and then right along the side of the wood. At the end of the wood, keep the hedge on your right and as it swings round to the left follow it by a horse jump. Descend to Mather Wood via a well-made footbridge, and aim for the right-hand corner of the wood where a waymarked arrow shows the path along the side of the field. The well-ridden path in front of you heads in the same direction and is easier underfoot, but it is not a recognised right of way.

(3) These paths converge by a small footbridge and yellow waymarker, where we turn right and then left along the fringe of the wood. The path is marked as heading across the field of rape seed plants, but unless you have a flamethrower it seems sensible to follow the apparent diversion around the edge. Keep the wood on your left as you go round the edge of the field. Turn right at Coppice Wood's end with a hedge now on your left, follow the left-hand turn of the hedge, and turn right just after the electric cables. As the hedge ends, a yellow waymark points the way left over a nettle shrouded footbridge, where a second arrow leads through more nettles.

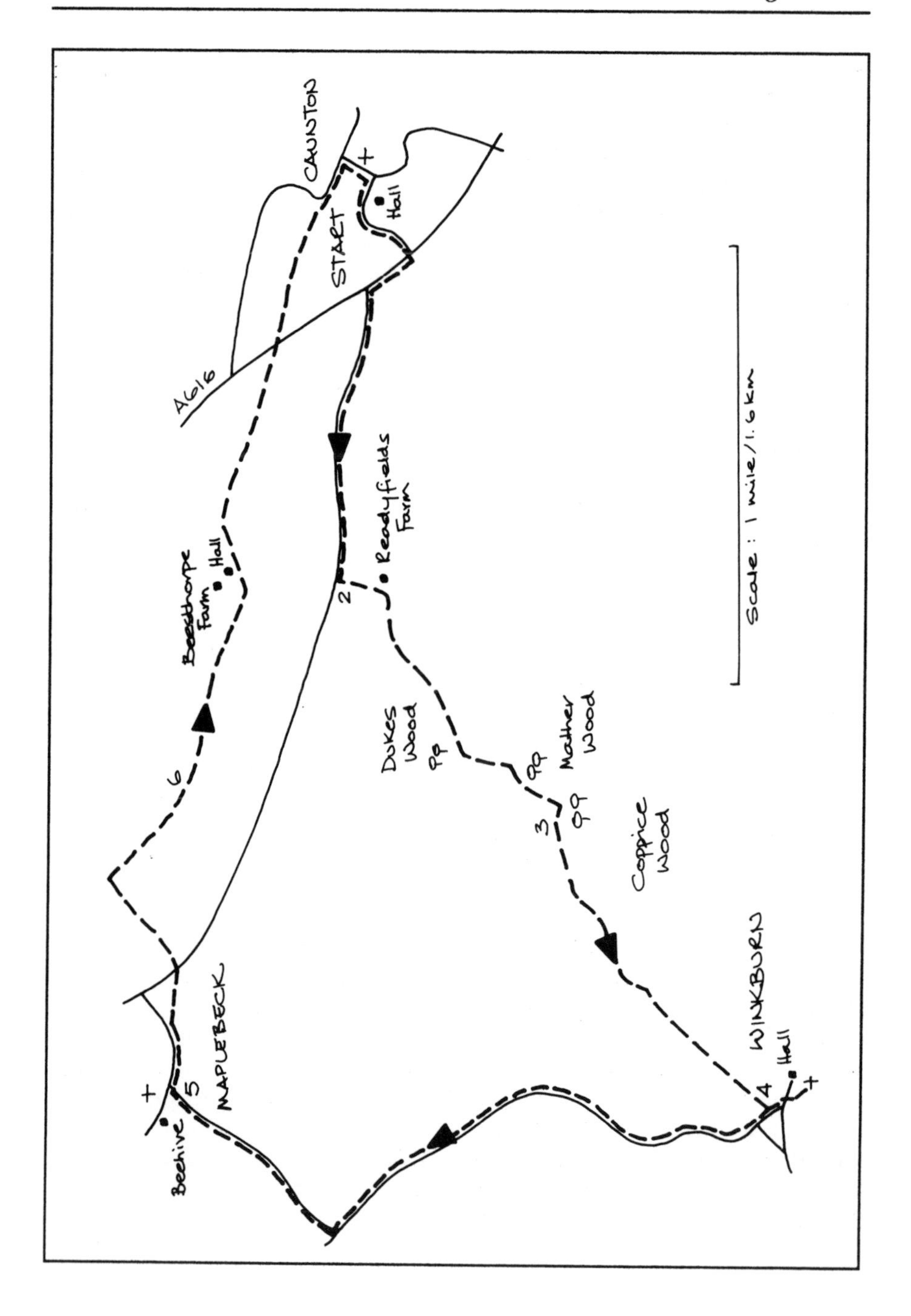
CAUNTON
Hall
START
A616
2
Readyfields Farm
Beesthorpe Farm
Hall
Dukes Wood
Mather Wood
3
Coppice Wood
WINKBURN
Hall
4
MAPLEBECK
5
Beehive
6
Scale : 1 mile/1.6 km

The path is obvious by the side of the field with yet another hawthorn hedge on your left, and you follow it towards the houses of Winkburn. Eventually a gravel road looms up on the left, and you follow it to the village past the farm buildings of the Hall. The road becomes metalled as the houses are reached, and passes an old closed public lavatory.

(4) At the corner turn left along the private drive towards the Hall, taking the footpath in front of you that goes slightly to the right towards the church. The church of St. John dates back to Norman times, and with the surrounding lands belonged to the Knights Hospitaller of St John of Jerusalem. This is the oldest Order of Chivalry and was formed to protect pilgrims on the way to the Holy Land. At the Dissolution of the Monasteries the lands were given to Thomas Burnell, Auditor to Henry VIII, and the memorials to him and his descendants decorate the lovely box-pewed church. A leaflet in the church will till you more about the history, and postcards are available for a modest donation. Be generous.

Return to the road after admiring the beautiful trees, and continue along it. Ignore the left-hand road by the bus shelter, and go past the post box. The road bends right and left, and after about a mile a footpath appears through a gap in the hedge on the right. Unfortunately this eventually leads into an impassable jungle of rape plants, and although it would be navigable in Winter, it is better to stick to the road. The reason for this is that after the next bend you encounter Maplebeck Viewpoint, where a plinth indicates the surprisingly good view. A profusion of wild flowers is carefully nurtured by the picnic area (with table), and it is a good spot to stop for a while. Carry on down the road to Maplebeck, turning left at the bottom to the Beehive.

(5) After quenching your thirst, return to the bus shelter, and if time permits have a look at the church. Take the main road out of the village, and as it bends left, a gate on your right indicates the well-trodden path. Cross the field and the stile opposite to emerge on the Caunton road. Turn right, then almost immediately left through a double gate by a footpath sign and waymarker. Follow the good track over a stream and head virtually straight on to a large oak tree in the corner of the field ahead. Turn right along the edge of the field and follow it with the hedge on your left. Skirt a meadow and rape field, always heading straight towards Beesthorpe farm, and then pass through old gate posts with a vandalised yellow waymarker.

The Beehive

(6) Follow the hedge to your right, pass two waymarkers on a post and as a hedge joins from the left, turn left and follow it. It is easy to miss this turn as a path also follows the right-hand hedge, but it is not a right of way. After 15 metres, a well-worn path on the right leads through the old join of two fields, and emerges at the track to the farm. Go straight on down this track, and after coming to the wood, climb the stile on the left by the footpath sign. Follow the waymarked path half right to a hedge, but do not go through the cut hole as it is private. Turn right and skirt the hall by the edge of the mown area to the old driveway, which you take to the right.

After 100 metres a white marker shows the re-routed footpath to the right, which you can follow to a stile. Cross the stile and turn left towards the house.

This field contained bullocks, which, whilst frisky and curious, may be dissuaded from following you by judicious language and gesture. Should you wish to avoid the encounter, return to the driveway and proceed down it to Caunton by minor roads.

The intrepid should go past the bullocks and house, and leave the field by a gate. Cross the road and the stile opposite, and follow the sheep track towards the church tower. On the left an old windmill has been converted to housing, and on the right the cricket ground comes into view. Ignore a new stile on the left, aiming for the corner of the field and its plank stile. Pass some conifers, cross a stile, pass the house to its right and go through a gate to the road. Turn right, pass Ford Lane and then take the next right at Main Road to the Plough and the bus shelter. The Plough serves Marston's Pedigree, and is a smart Inn with a good selection of food. Outside tables add to its attraction.

20. PLEASLEY HILL

Route: Pleasley Hill – Radmanthwaite – Little Matlock – Littlewood – Sunnydale – Northfield Lane – West Sidings – Pleasley Hill.

Distance: 5 miles

Map: O.S. Pathfinder 779 (Mansfield North)

Start: The Old Plough Inn, Pleasley Hill (Grid Reference 507642)

Access: There's a good daily bus service from Mansfield, Chesterfield and Sheffield. Travel on the A617 from Chesterfield, the M1 or Mansfield. Plenty of roadside parking close to the pub.

Ye Olde Plough, Pleasley Hill (0623 810386)

Ye Olde Plough was built in 1859 as a roadside inn and has been tastefully modernised in recent years, including the use of real oak wood in the furnishings and stained glass windows especially commissioned for the pub. The inn offers a warm welcome for the walker and is open all day Monday to Saturdays and usual Sunday hours. Food is served at lunch and evening as well as a range of cask beers including Ansells Mild, Tetley Bitter, Burton Ale and Mansfields Old Baily plus two guest beers! There is seating outside and families are welcome.

On the border between Nottinghamshire and Derbyshire, Pleasley Hill is a modern development to the medieval settlement of Pleasley on the other side of the valley. Coal mining during the last century brought the rapid development of the village that was described as a mere hamlet in the 1880s.

The Walk

(1) From the pub, walk left towards the traffic lights and cross the A617 road there. On the other side of the road go left to the flight of steps leading up through the retaining wall on your right. These mark the route of the footpath, but some considerate soul has completely blocked the top of the steps with a pile of brushwood, so continue along the road for a short distance. A lane leads off on the right and immediately forks. A footpath sign directs you left and a sign on the right proclaims that this is a private road. Go right! Ascend the lane and leave the main road and its noise behind. Where the lane bends left, there is another pile of brushwood, for this marks the top of the steps you saw earlier. Continue along the lane, climbing steadily. The lane has hedges on both sides, but now and then there are gaps and you can see across Pleasley Vale to the old parish church and the colliery buildings. These of course are in Derbyshire, for the county boundary is the stream in the valley bottom.

(2) As you approach the farm buildings of Radmanthwaite, fringed by Scots Pines, there is a green gate across the lane. Just to the left of the gate is a stile in the wall. Go over this stile and into a small paddock. The exit stile is directly opposite, alongside another gate. This stile takes you into a much larger field, the far boundary of which cannot be seen. The field is also home to several horses, but unlike some, these seem docile. An obvious path, which seems to owe its existence more to the horses than to human feet, heads across the field to the left of a pile of stones, in the general direction of a chimney with a conical top. The "path" peters out, but continue to head for the chimney and soon a stile comes into view in the far corner of the field.

(3) The stile, which is waymarked, gives access onto a former railway line, now converted into a walking route. Turn right along the old railway route. The railway was built by the Midland Railway Company in the 1870's to serve the various pits between Mansfield Woodhouse and Westhouses on the Sheffield – Nottingham Line. It was a belated attempt to stave off competition from the rival Great Northern Railway, but it failed to prevent that company constructing an almost parallel route on the opposite side of the valley. Thus Pleasley once had two stations, but now has none.

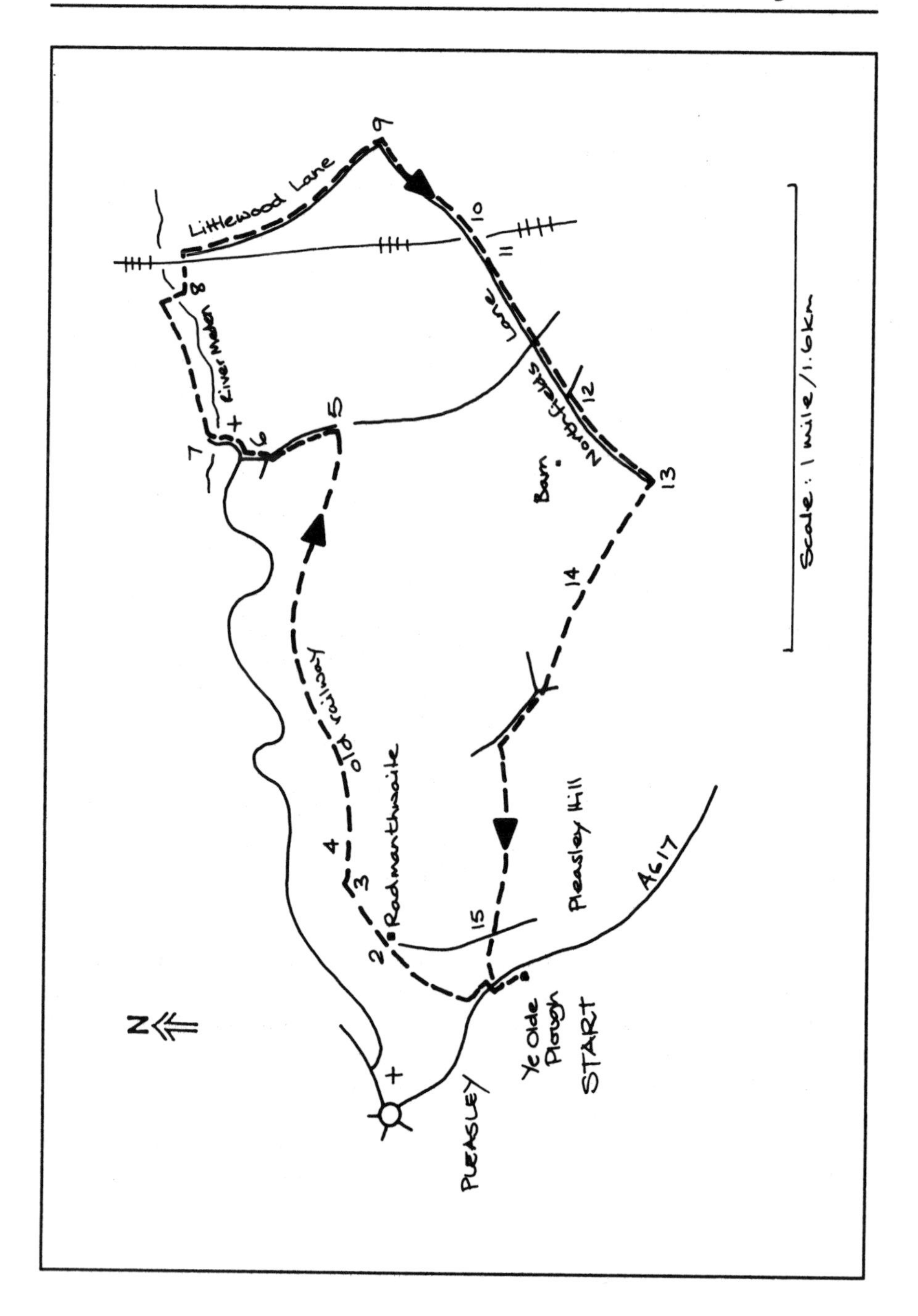
Littlewood Lane
9
10
11
12
13
14
15
8
7
6
5
4
3
2
River Meden
old railway
Radmanthwaite
Northfield Lane
Barn
Pleasley Hill
A617
Ye Olde Plough
START
PLEASLEY
N
Scale: 1 mile/1.6km

(4) The railway is a delightful walk, with a veritable riot of vegetation cloaking the embankment and cutting sides. The conical topped chimney, seen earlier, is soon passed on the left and there are the remains of sidings that once served the factory. The sidings are gone and the factory too is derelict. The line passes through a fine rock cutting and under a bridge before the views open out and there is an orchard on the left. All too soon the track dips to a little car park and the road. The railway continued to a junction at Mansfield Woodhouse, but this section is not walkable.

(5) At the road go left, noting the sign which proclaims that the road ahead is closed at the barrier and wondering whether there has been some political coup d'etat which has resulted in the Derbyshire/ Nottinghamshire border being closed. You'll find the barrier open more often than not. Anyhow there is nothing to stop pedestrians avoiding the barrier, no barbed wire entanglements, no minefields, no watch towers or gun emplacements, just a perfectly normal country lane. Ignore the track leading into the factory and eventually you'll reach a point where the lane forks. The route to the left is signed as a 'No Through Road', so bear right noting the fine terrace of stone houses on the left. As you come level with the terrace, there is another lane leading off to the right. Follow this at it continues to descend towards the valley bottom.

(6) At the bottom of the hill the lane broadens out. On the right is the well-hidden church of St Chad. Ahead are various notices proclaiming that the land is private, so go left and cross over the bridge which spans the River Meden and so enter Derbyshire. Just on the Derbyshire side of the bridge is another gate proclaiming that the way ahead is private, but on the right is a stile and this takes you into open fields.

(7) The map shows this place as Little Matlock and the reason for this is soon apparent. As the path winds obviously through the field, a line of limestone crags appears on the left. Although by Matlock standards they are small, nevertheless they offer some interesting scrambles and are the playground of budding climbers. At the end of the crags there is a stile, and the well-blazed path goes through another field on quite a distinct terrace before reaching yet another stile and a track. Here go right, along the track, which soon crosses the Meden again and so re-enters Nottinghamshire. This is Littlewood Bridge.

(8) Beyond the bridge the track bears left and soon forks. Keep to the left-hand fork to pass underneath the railway line and then follow the lane round to the right to ascend to the level of the railway. This is Littlewood Lane and it is fringed with a plethora of hawthorn and crab apples. The lane soon bears left, away from the railway. The map shows a triangular field between the lane and the railway line, but this turns out to be inaccurate as there is a deep and abandoned quarry! There are various warning notices which should be heeded, even if the legality of the wording is open to doubt. Soon the first houses of Mansfield Woodhouse come into view and shortly afterwards the track disgorges onto the edge of a housing estate.

(9) Go right here, past the modern bungalows, heading for the old farm buildings which are ahead. Keep straight on, ignoring roads going off to the left. The route is a curious mixture of road and track, but at the entrance to Sunnydale Farm, it decides to be a track and rises steadily to cross the Mansfield – Worksop Railway.

(10) The bridge is not of the best design; functional would be the best description. Nevertheless it is of interest, if only because it also spans the trackbed of the line on which you were walking earlier, for this was the junction of the two railways. The erstwhile line to Pleasley can be seen curving away to the left, only now it has been converted into a road!

(11) The track, here known as Northfield Lane, continues alongside fields on the right and a car cemetery on the left, to reach a tarred drive where the access to North Lodge trails in from the right. Keep straight on and soon reach a cross roads. Here again there are the curious signs implying that the road on the right is closed. Even more unusual is the 25 mph sign. Ignore all these and continue straight on along Northfield Lane, which here is a proper road again. Note particularly on the left the restoration work going on the colliery spoil heap. Already the heap has been planed down and there are trees growing on parts of it. A few more years and it will be unrecognisable.

(12) At the white houses, Northfield Avenue goes off, sharp left, but you continue ahead along a narrowing track, which then widens at a set of gates. Ignore the gates and go up the narrow path. This is still Northfield Lane and it is a lovely survival of a green lane, being closely hemmed in with very mixed hedgerows and fully grown trees. The name suggests

the medieval open field system and away to the right, across the field, you may glimpse the ruins of the ancient Northfield Barn.

(13) At the top of the hill, the hedge on the right gives way to a fence and shortly afterwards the track turns abruptly left. Do not go this way however, but turn right, through a gap in the fence and set off across the field. The way ahead is usually very distinct, for these paths are well walked, but in case you need directions, the route heads towards the second pylon to the right of the chimney. The chimney is that of Pleasley Colliery and it is a most useful marker. The more obvious derelict metal barn is no use at all as a guide. There is a good view back from here over Mansfield Woodhouse, to the twin headgear of Clipstone Colliery. For all the mention of industry and coal-mines, this area is surprisingly rural and very pleasant easy walking.

(14) The walk across the field ends at a stile in the hedge. Negotiate this and bear right, going diagonally across the field. Again the route is clear, and again the chimney is a good guide. The path heads towards a point mid-way between the two pylons to the right of the chimney. A stile in the hedge at the corner of the field leads into a lane. Go right here, but where the lane turns right towards West Sidings, go through the second gate on the left – it is waymarked and there is also a stile. The path follows the hedge on the left until the corner of the field is reached. Corner is perhaps too strong a term; bend would be more appropriate. At the point where the hedge bends to the right there are two stiles close together on the left, both waymarked. You want the second, which takes you into another field. Here the path runs alongside a hedge again, but the hedge is now on your right. The path gently ascends the slope to another stile in the top right-hand corner of the field. There are two waymarks here. Ignore the one pointing left, which only takes you down through the playing fields, and instead bear right, heading for the Pleasley chimney again. As before, the path is well used and you would find it difficult to go astray. A stile in the hedge at the opposite side of the field drops you into a narrow lane. This is an alternative access to Radmanthwaite Farm that you passed at the start of the walk. The "thwaite" element of this place name is pure Norse, meaning "a piece of reclaimed land." Interestingly, the Radmanthwaite name occurs three times in this area.

(15) Cross the lane and go over the stile opposite into fields again. The path is waymarked, but who needs waymarks when you have a colliery chimney for a guide post. Down the field you go, to a gap in the bottom right-hand corner. The rumble of traffic on the A617 can now be heard, and the pub is below, on the left through the trees. The path goes steeply down among the trees to reach a flight of steps. These descend even more steeply to the left and disgorge onto the footway by the A617, only a stone's throw from the Old Plough. Cross the road with great care to reach the front door of the pub and a well earned drink.

Ye Olde Plough

21. WELLOW

Route: Wellow Green – Wellow Dam – Kirton Brickworks – Laxton Common – Wellow Green

Distance: 5 miles (mainly woodland)

Map: O.S. Pathfinder 780 (Ollerton)

Start: Wellow Green (Grid reference SK 670662)

Access: Wellow is 1.5 miles south of Ollerton on the A 616 to Newark. There is a regular bus from Mansfield via Ollerton, East Midlands No. 13, and the Travel Wright No. 32, Ollerton – Newark, stops here. These are part of the Sherwood Forester Network. Car drivers should note that there is very limited parking in Wellow and it may be necessary to use the Wellow Dam car park.

The Olde Red Lion, Wellow (0623 861000)

This is a beautifully restored pub dating back to 1600, encompassing the original one room inn and a row of labourers' cottages. The result is a series of cosy rooms of character, featuring old photographs and drawings of the green with its maypole. This free house offered excellent beers from Websters, Boddingtons and Ruddles at the time of our visit, and the extensive menu of over 20 main meals included five vegetarian dishes. There is an outside beer garden and children's area, and bookings are taken for weekend meals in the No Smoking dining area. Opening times are from 11.30am until 3pm and from 5.30pm in the evening.

Durham Ox, Wellow

This John Smith pub serves Ruddles, Courage Director's and Tetley's as well as the brewery bitter. It has an extensive menu, children's play area and in addition is open all day on Saturday.

Wellow

Wellow is a conservation village that dates to pre-Saxon times, when it was known as *Wellah.* The surrounding earthworks are now preserved under the Ancient Monuments Act, but the most striking feature of the village is its Maypole on the green. It was renewed in 1977 to mark the Queen's Silver Jubilee, and each Whit Monday Bank Holiday is the centre of the celebrations for hundreds of people. One of only three permanent Maypoles in the country, it is 66 feet high – the length of a cricket pitch. Whether this indicates a pagan origin to the game is for you to decide. The church of St. Swithin's dates back to the late 12th Century, and, although heavily restored in 1878, has a certain squat charm. Both of the pubs have character, and the interesting variety of houses around the village green make it an excellent place to end a walk or for an evening visit.

The Walk

(1) From the maypole, head down to the main road and turn left along the pavement in front of the Durham Ox. Just after the bend, aim slightly right on a faint path to the corner of the Wellow Dam lake. The pond used to have a ducking stool, but now anglers' lines are the only objects being submerged. Steer towards the right of the water, head briefly in the direction of Park Farm, but then turn left by the yellow waymark on the telegraph pole. Follow the dirt road, with the pond on

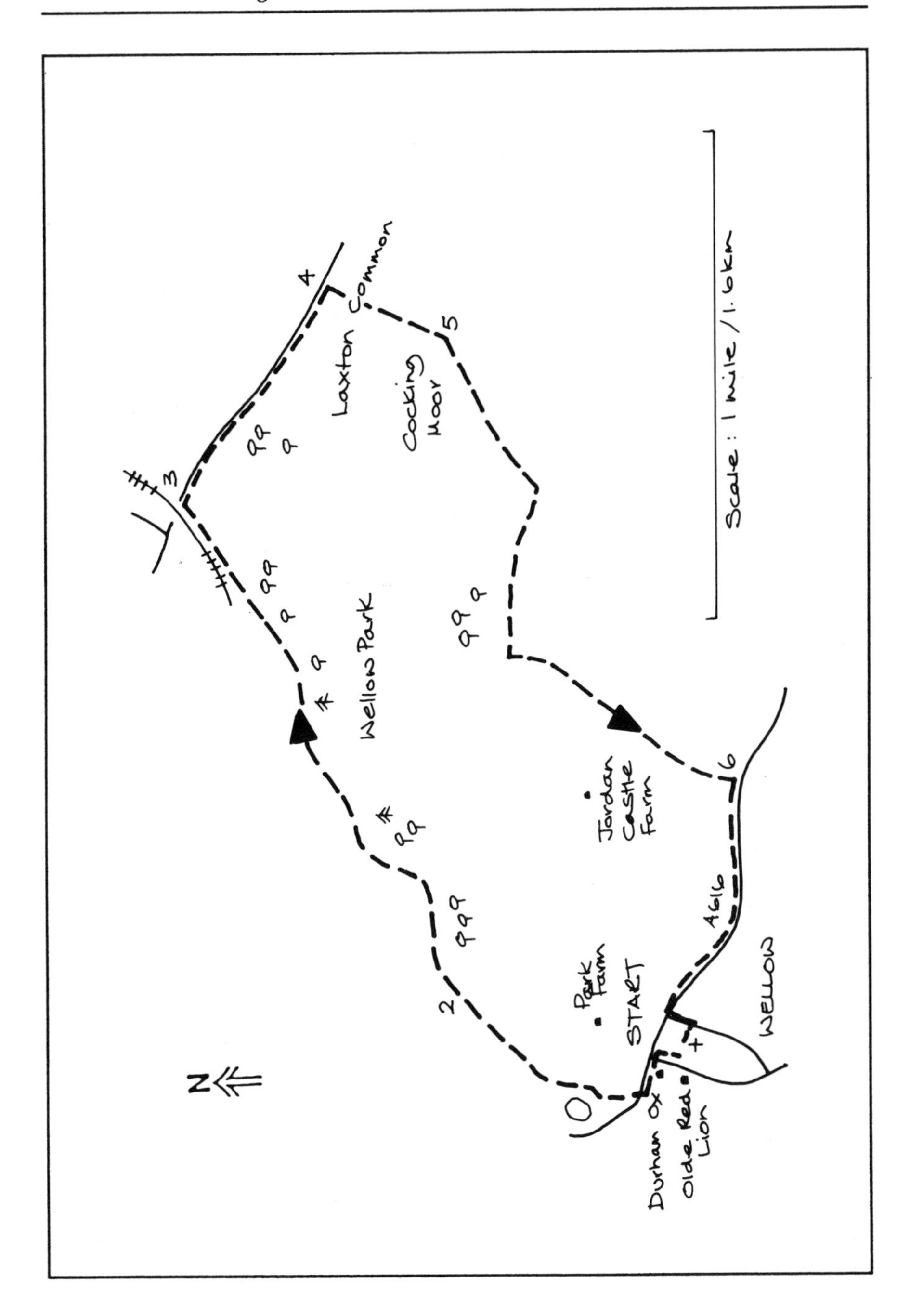
Scale : 1 mile / 1.6km
N
Laxton Common
Cocking Moor
Wellow Park
Jordan Castle Farm
Park Farm
START
A616
WELLOW
Durham Ox
Olde Red Lion
2
3
4
5
6

your left, as it bears to the right between hedgerows. The track shows signs of having been improved by old rubble, and gradually joins the lower slopes of Wellow Park's woodland.

(2) Pass a yellow waymarker to your right and follow the obvious track through the woodland. Soon a sign proclaiming this to be Forestry Commission land with pedestrian access only is encountered, with an accompanying fence to discourage bikes and horses. Proceed onwards, under a delightful mixture of Oak, Beech and Birch, with many wild flowers by the edge of the path. The deep red of the soil is exposed in many places, and it can be wet and muddy in parts. Ignore a track from the right, which is part of the network used by the tree-felling vehicles, and continue past a second barrier. The track becomes quite rutted as you leave the wood and approach the brickworks now visible in front of you.

(3) At the road turn right and walk up the hill towards Laxton. Laxton is a unique village as it still practises the open field medieval farming system. It has a walking trail, leaflets on which are available from the Sherwood Forest Visitors Centre or local Tourist Information Offices, and it was also the site of an old Motte and Bailey. At the top of the hill ignore the path into Wellow Park, and don't waste time looking for the footpath on the right, which is marked on the map, as it has been long commandeered by the crops. Follow the road for a further 250 metres across Laxton Common, turning right at a wooden Public Bridlepath signpost.

(4) Follow the straight path by a small ditch until it enters the woodland of Cocking Moor.

(5) After 100 yards a pair of blue waymark arrows are reached, and a bridleway joins from the left. Those wishing a longer walk can turn left here and follow the obvious track to Shortwood Farm, Ompton, and then South West across the fields to a point at Grid Reference 675643.

Return to Wellow by the minor road past the pumping station, adding about 2 miles to the walk. Otherwise carry on through this stretch of woodland, with the path bearing right as it becomes reinforced by cinders and what looks like old tarmac. The track swings to the left as you emerge from the woodland into a hawthorn-fringed lane, well-used by horses. To the right Jordan Castle farm and its outbuildings come into view, although no sign is apparent of the old earthworks of the 13th Century castle. Continue down this recently restored track, ignoring any gates or side turnings, until it peters out into a narrow grass path just before the A 616.

(6) At the road turn right, watching out for the traffic. Some half a mile to the left you will see the curious-pyramid shaped roofs of the Ompton Boreholes pumping station. Follow the road into Wellow by the pavement on the right. Note the old moat of Gorge Dyke after you have entered the village to either side of the road. Continue down to the Durham Ox, or preferably turn left up Potters Lane, then right into the churchyard, leaving it by the paved path to the Red Lion. The church contains three old bells that are rung every September 19th. This is in gratitude for the safe deliverance of Lady Walden, a visitor 200 years ago who became lost in the woods before managing to return by following the sound of the bells.

22. WALESBY

Route: Walesby – Haughton – Bothamstall – Conjure Alders – Walesby

Distance: 7 miles (Excellent tracks, roads)

Map: O.S. Pathfinder 763 (Clumber Park and East Markham)

Start: Red Lion, Walesby. (Grid reference SK 684707)

Access: East Midlands 34 Retford – New Ollerton, approximately hourly. Some buses connect to Nottingham. Also the 15 Mansfield – Walesby via Ollerton, approximately every hour. It is on the Sherwood Forester network. Travel on the B6387 from Ollerton to Walesby. Car parking available in the village.

Carpenter's Arms, Walesby (0623 860716)

This pub lies just outside the village but is well worth the diversion. The Carpenters serves a fine pint of Everards beers-Beacon, Tiger and Original. The pub is open from noon to 3pm and from 7pm in the evening on Mondays to Saturday evenings. Usual Sunday hours prevail. Food is served at all sessions and families are welcome.

Red Lion, Walesby

While in the village, why not try The Red Lion too? This serves Mansfield beers in the smaller lounge or large public bar. It is an old fashioned local that opens at lunchtimes and evenings throughout the week. Usual Sunday hours are observed.

Walesby

Not an outstanding village, but the church of St Edmund is worth a look. Unusually, it has glass fibre tower pinnacles. The Vicars of Walesby are listed inside from 1257, since when they have also been responsible for Haughton Chapel about which a leaflet may be bought, and whose ruins we shall pass later.

The other claim to fame is the scout camp, a gift from C.Pearson and the National Fitness Council in 1938 to the Notts Scout Association, which is used by thousands of youngsters each year.

The Red Lion

The Walk

(1)With your back to the Red Lion, turn left up Main Street and then right at the top along Tuxford Road. Turn left up Green Lane after visiting the church, cross a bridlepath and follow the grassy track as it goes to the right by Robin Hood Way and yellow circular walk markers on a post. Turn right along a tractor road at the end of the right-hand hedge, and after 400 yards turn left by a line of trees. Follow the path by the trees, and when it bends to the right, cross the stile in the hedge in front of you. Turn left over the stile along a well worn farm track which then turns right.

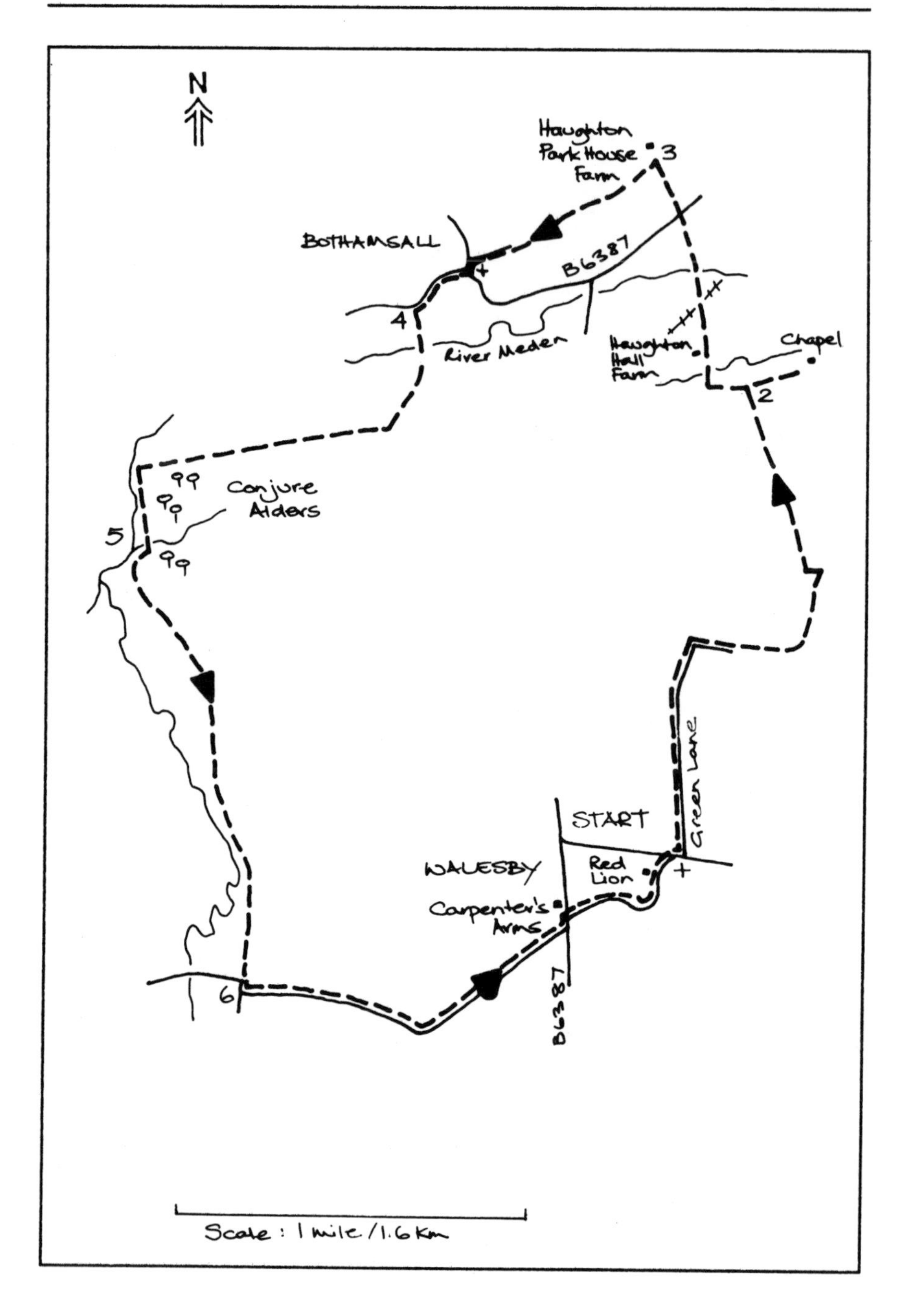
N
Haughton
Park House
Farm
3
BOTHAMSALL
B6387
4
River Meden
Haughton
Hall
Farm
Chapel
2
Conjure
Alders
5
Green Lane
START
WALESBY
Red
Lion
Carpenter's
Arms
B6387
6
Scale: 1 mile/1.6 Km

(2) After 500 yards, as your path turns left, follow a similar track right towards the National Mining Museum at Lound Hall. 200 yards down the lane a fenced area on the left denotes the overgrown ruins of Haughton Chapel, now sadly decayed from its Norman splendour. A memorial to our own mortality.

King John granted this along with Walesby Church to the Abbey at Rouen in Normandy, and it was the burial place for the Stanhope and Holles families when they lived at Haughton Hall. The Holles became the Dukes of Newcastle, and it seems that everywhere you go in this area lies a ruin that used to belong to them. Haughton Hall itself was demolished in 1770 and its foundations form the base of the farm of the same name.

Return along the track, pass the path we came along and turn right over the River Maun by Haughton Hall Farm. Go under the railway bridge for Bevercotes Colliery, the world's first push-button pit, cross the B6387 road and turn left by Haughton Park House Farm with its most unusual facade and cupola.

(3) Here we leave the Robin Hood Way, although the thirsty may continue down it to the pub at Elkesley. The way to Bothamstall is obvious and straight, and we pass through three gates in the company of birds, butterflies and delicious blackberries in season. Enter the village, passing Church Farm on our right where two old cannons mark the entrance, and emerge by St Peter's Church. Many Mansells are buried in the graveyard, but I could not find a Nigel.

Follow the main road in front of you past the Village Hall in the sadly pub-less conservation village of Bothamstall, and turn left downhill just after The Homestead and a monstrous greenhouse.

(4) The metalled road becomes a dirt track and crosses the Medan by a good viewpoint and lunchstop. To the left of the village a conspicuous tree-covered mound can be seen, a man-made site of an old Motte and Bailey Castle, whilst a more modern construction of a pond is pleasing on the other side.

Continue along the track, turn left as it rejoins the Medan by a tremendous stretch of trees known as Conjure Alders. This takes its name from Conigswath or Kings Ford, marking where the ancient road from Blyth to Wellow crossed the rivers as it followed the edge of the forest of Sherwood. This is the road that we will now follow for a couple of miles.

(5) Cross the footbridge, turn right past the weir and ignore the next bridge which replaces the old ford. Turn left through the woods and Indian balsam, following blue waymarkers along the sandy road eroded by centuries of travel. Pass a potato field on your left and eventually emerge to the open grasslands of the Scout Camp. Take the right-hand path along the edge of the woodland and follow it towards the river, which you meet by an outcrop of sandstone and Robin Hood's cave. Keep going straight on one of the many paths to emerge at a road.

(6) Turn left and walk the mile to Walesby. You enter the village by the Carpenters Arms, which boasts a playground, beer garden and excellent beers on hand-pump. It has an extensive menu and on a sunny day is perhaps a better bet than the Red Lion. Why not just cross over the main road, walk the 400 metres and make your own comparison?

23. NETHER LANGWITH

Route: Nether Langwith – Blue Barn Farm – Pasture Hill Farm – Langwith Mill – Cuckney Hay Wood – Boon Hills Wood – Top Farm – Nether Langwith

Distance: 4 miles

Map: Pathfinder Nos. 762 (Worksop South) and 779 (Mansfield North)

Start: Limes Avenue, Nether Langwith. Limited parking at the junction with the track to Blue Barn Farm (Grid Reference SK 534707)

Access: There are daily bus services from Mansfield and Bolsover. Travel by car on the A632 from Cuckney, Bolsover or Chesterfield. Limes Avenue is right on the eastern edge of Nether Langwith.

The Jug and Glass, Nether Langwith (0623 742283)

The delightfully-situated old coaching inn, The Jug and Glass lies just by the junction of the A632 and Limes Avenue. It is an enterprising free house which offers a continuously changing range of cask conditioned beers. The pub fronts the stream and despite the proximity of the main road it is a very pleasant place to sit outside and watch the world go by. In summer, the pub is often the scene of local events such as Morris Dancing and the annual plastic duck race in June. Families are welcome and food is served all week. Bookings are required on Sundays. The Jug and Glass is open from 11am until 5.30pm Mondays to Saturdays in the summer, until 3.30pm in Winter. It reopens at 7pm in the evenings. Usual Sunday hours.

Nether Langwith

This traditional mining community on the edge of the Dukeries grew up around the village during the last century. Nearby is the picturesque village of Cuckney and Welbeck Abbey founded by Thomas de Cuckney.

The Jug and Glass

The Walk

(1) From the pub, walk up Limes Avenue to the point where it swings left. On the right is a track which leads to Blue Barn Farm. This track is followed towards the farm without any difficulty. Where the track turns right near to the farm, go straight on, through a stile, which is waymarked, and so enter fields. The Pathfinder map shows the right of way running alongside the left-hand side of the field to the metal gate in the corner then turning right alongside the hedge. This is not what happens in practice, for there is a beaten path bearing right and cutting across the field to a stile in the opposite hedge. On reaching this stile you should ignore it and continue to the right, to a kissing gate in the wall. This takes you out onto a track again, just beyond Blue Barn Farm.

(2) Continue along the track away from the farm, passing the covert on the left. Again there are no route-finding problems, simply a question of following the rough lane that soon dips, then climbs slightly. At the wooden electricity pole, another track goes off to the right. Go right here

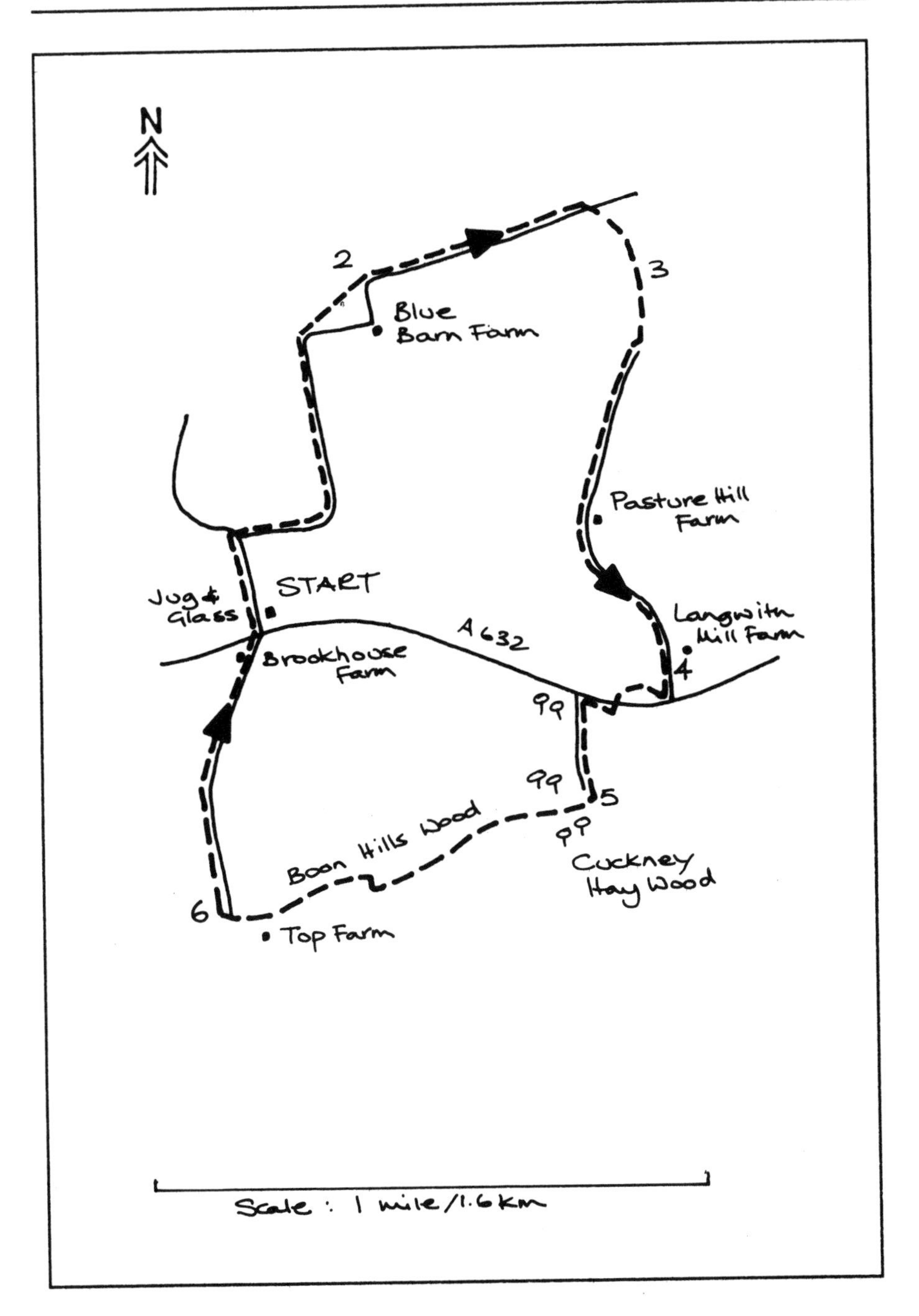
N
2
3
Blue
Barn Farm
Pasture Hill
Farm
START
Jug &
Glass
A 632
Langwith
Mill Farm
4
Brookhouse
Farm
5
Boon Hills Wood
Cuckney
Hay Wood
6
Top Farm
Scale : 1 mile/1.6 km

and leave the lane. A short distance along this next track you will reach a waymarked gate. Beyond it the track continues, but your route lies through the gate, then right, through the broad gap in the hedge, thus leaving the track behind. In the field, head diagonally left to reach a gate and stile in the far corner. Neither gate nor stile are visible from the gap where you enter the field, nor is there much evidence of a path on the ground. The approach to the gate is very muddy and it looks as if, at one time, there may have been a pond on the right.

(3) Go over the stile and, keeping the hedge on your right. Follow the indistinct path to reach another gate and stile. This takes you into a narrow, rough lane and so to Pasture Hill Farm. The lane skirts to the right of the farm buildings, but it can be atrociously muddy and the two gates near the farm were most reluctant to open. Ignore the stile on the right near to the second gate and continue down the lane towards the old mill buildings.

(4) At Langwith Mill, which is now converted to a restaurant, the lane bears right and ascends quite steeply to join the main A632 road. An improvement some years ago has left the old road intact but unused. This is a fortunate chance for the walker. Go right here along the old road until it peters out, then cross to the far side of the A632, where there is a footway. Continue along the main road for a short distance, until the left-hand bend is reached, by the wood. There is a decrepit seat here, but it is not the best of places to sit, being too close to the road for comfort. Go up the rough track on the left by the seat. Where the track forks, keep straight on and shortly enter Cuckney Hay Wood.

(5) The path in the wood is well defined and rises slowly through the trees to an open area where a number of tracks meet. Go right here and soon the path reaches the edge of the woodland, with open fields on the left and the trees on the right. At the end of the wood the path crosses a track and continues through fields, with the hedge on the left. At the far end of the field there is a double stile of unusual construction, for it links two fields and a strip of woodland. Your way is into the trees. The path bears right in the trees, with open land to the left until the corner of the fence is reached. Here the path goes left, still on the edge of Boon Hills Wood, until a stile is reached, close to Boon Hills Top Farm. The stile disgorges onto a track and here you go right and descend through the wood.

(6) The track soon leaves the wood and turns right. Nether Langwith can now be seen ahead and the only obstacle is likely to be mud, especially if there has been recent heavy rain. Continue on the track, passing to the right of Brook House Farm to emerge on the A632 again, directly opposite Limes Avenue and the Jug and Glass.

24. EAST MARKHAM

Route: East Markham – Milton – Bevercotes – West Markham – East Markham

Distance: 4.5 or 7 miles (Roads, Good paths)

Map: O.S. Pathfinder 763 Clumber Park and East Markham

Start: Bus shelter on Hall Lane, East Markham. (Grid reference SK 743730)

Access: East Markham lies just off the A1, above Tuxford. Car parking is possible at various points in the village. East Midlands Bus 34 Retford – Ollerton passes through roughly hourly, and there are connections to Nottingham. It is part of the Sherwood Forester Network.

Queens Hotel, East Markham

An interesting pub whose lounge has a very homely feel. It currently sells an excellent pint of Adnams on hand-pump, but the landlord is hoping to extend his cellar soon to enable him to increase his range of real ales. The dining area is nicely offset, and serves a good variety of tempting foods that are always available during opening hours. As a bonus the pub is open from 11 to 11, Monday to Saturday, and situated near to bus stops. Normal Sunday hours. There is a beer garden behind the car park, and children are welcome.

East Markham

Originally this was the main town of the area, but in 1609 a plague wiped out 115 people, more than a quarter of the population, leading to a rise in importance for the town of Tuxford. The Markham family, who took their name from the town, produced several notable persons. Judge Markham drew up the instruments for deposing of Richard II, enabling Henry Bolingbroke to become King. His son John Markham was known as the Upright Judge. He received special praise from Henry IV for sending the Prince of Wales to jail after the latter had struck the judge for refusing to free one of the Prince's servants. The Markham family tree can be found in St John the Baptist's Church, which also has an exquisite brass of Millicent Mering, the tomb of the Judge and a selection of cards and tea-towels for sale. Markham Hall contains little of the old Hall, and dates from 1777.

The Walk

(1) From the bus shelter on Hall Lane, turn right towards the Hall behind its tall wall, and then take the first left down Church Street. Note how many houses are built gable end to the road, a feature of the area that dates back 1500 years; it was introduced to make best use of the high ground in the boggy areas before drainage in the 18th Century. The fine 15th Century perpendicular style church of St John may be entered by the North door and is well worth the look. Leave the churchyard and continue right down Church Street, taking the first left up Plantation Road. This may refer to the history of Markham as a fruit growing area, with 200 tons of Plums being sent by rail alone in 1886.

On your left East Markham Pinfold is an ancient monument, a pinfold being a place where cattle were gathered together. Carry straight on at the two road junctions to the Queens Hotel on your right, and, suitably refreshed continue down the road to the Crown Inn. This, by the way, also has a selection of real beers including Courage Directors, John Smiths and Websters, a small garden and a good variety of food. It does, however, close between 3 and 5.30pm on a weekday.

Leave the pub, turn right and after 100 metres cross over the road and a stile by a yellow waymarker and footpath sign into a bullock field. After 40 metres a stile on the left is crossed, turning right along the fence. You deviate from the authorised path by going through a gate at the top left-hand corner of the field, and down the brick track cum driveway between bungalows to the road. The marked path involves negotiating the bullocks, which I for one was not prepared to do, and someone's back garden. Locals use the way described. At the road turn right, and right again up York Street. Should you wish to investigate the aforementioned path you will see a footpath sign on the right behind a rockery.

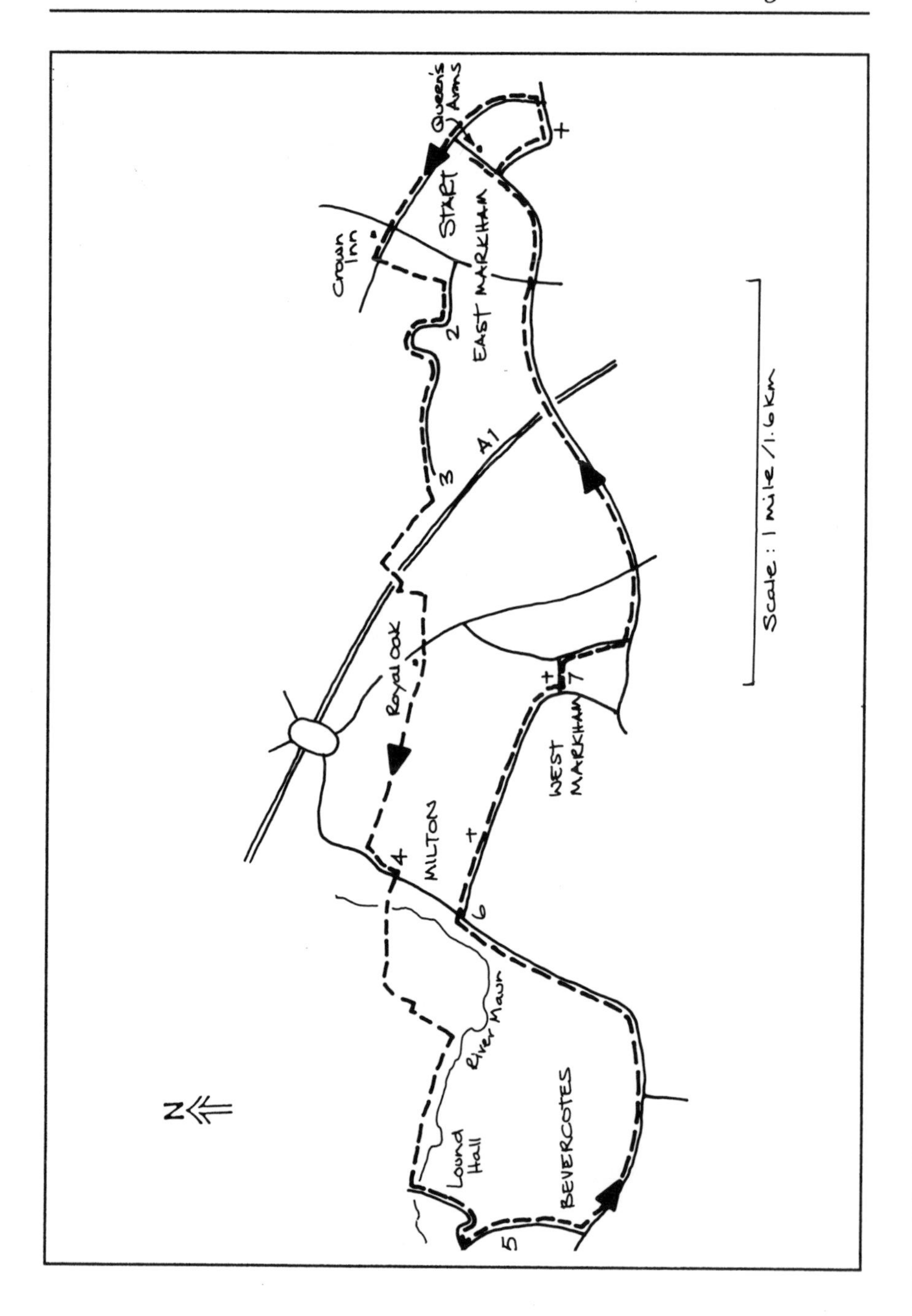

Queen's Arms
START
EAST MARKHAM
Crown Inn
2
3
A1
Royal Oak
4
MILTON
6
WEST MARKHAM
7
River Maun
Lound Hall
BEVERCOTES
5
N
Scale : 1 mile / 1.6 Km

(2) Continue past some odd-looking houses with flat roofs, and when the road turns right, go left up a mown grass strip between hedges and a white metallic gate that does not appear to have been closed for years. Ignore a footpath and sign to the left, and head right along the hedge. Cross another beautifully mown grass area, and carry on along the well trodden if nettly path. This becomes a lane, crosses a cornfield and goes through a gap in the hedge above the A1.

(3) Turn right on the obvious but overgrown path and after 250 metres drop down the steep embankment to the bridge over the A1. Cross the bridge and turn right at the main tractor road to the Royal Oak Inn. Just before the inn there is a bridlepath sign pointing left that indicates the next stage of the walk.

The Inn caters for the A1 traveller and is consequently posh and characterless. The small public bar offers Riding or Old Baily from handpumps, a good selection of food, and a pool table, while there are tables and a children's play area outside.

Go right up the bridlepath, leaving the old Great North Road, cross a footbridge and a large cornfield to emerge at a road. The odd dinosaur-like contraptions that you will have seen in front of you belong to Bevercotes Colliery, and we will get a closer look at them and the intriguing cupola of Milton Church to the left later. However, they may well be extinct due to pit closures. Turn left at the road and after 150 yards pause by the bridlepath sign on the right of the road to make a decision: do you put in the extra 2.5 mile loop via Lound Hall or get in more drinking time at the Queens by heading up the road and taking the first left at point (6) on the map? If the latter, skip the next two sections.

(4) Turn right up the bridleway, cross the River Maun, go through a gate and follow the track in front of you. At the next gate turn left between a hedge and a fence along another bridlepath, which after two turns goes through a pair of gates and turns right as the Maun is re-met. The obvious path crosses a footbridge and eventually turns left over the Maun to Lound Hall Training Centre and Mining Museum. Follow the arrow left as the tarmac is reached, and pass Ventilation, Conveyer Section and sundry mining equipment at the training centre.

(5) As the road is reached, turn right to visit the Museum if so desired; the walk continues left towards Bevercotes. Take the left fork by the pond, and left again at the next junction. A footpath is marked but it is hard to find and overgrown, so it is perhaps easier to continue down the road to Milton.

(6) Take the road uphill to the right along a Lime Tree framed avenue, rejoining those who missed out the loop. Soon Milton Church of All Saints emerges on the left and we enter the graveyard through an iron gate. This building is unfortunately closed due to disrepair, but was completed in 1831 as a Mausoleum and church to house the tomb of the Duchess of Newcastle; she died in 1822 giving birth to twins, her 13th confinement, at the age of 33. Designed by Sir Robert Smirke who was also the architect for the British Museum, it was possibly paid for out of the compensation received by the Duke when his Nottingham Castle was burnt by reformists. When this church was opened they closed the one in West Markham, but now the roles are reversed. The churchyard is still used, and interestingly graves of local families such as the Pierreponts and Whites may be seen in both places.

Continue up the road and then enter the grounds of Old Saints at West Markham, also known as Markham Clinton. The third church of the day is a fascinating contrast to the others, having Saxon style brickwork inside, a Norman doorway and Font, and East Anglian style weather-boarding on the tower. If locked, a key may be obtained locally.

(7) Leave the churchyard at the opposite end by the old school, currently the subject of a dispute as to its future. Also a Smythe building, there are objections to its conversion to a house. Turn right and then left along the road to East Markham. On the way you pass sadly faded photographs of badger, butterfly and hare, turning left by the fox. These are a nice touch to brighten up the village. Cross the Great North Road again, pass Cleveland Windmill (built in 1837), go straight across at the main road and travel down Mark Lane to the bus stops or car. Those returning to Ollerton can use the bus stop on the right by the main road and watch all the Poultry lorries go by.

25. ASKHAM

Route: Rockley – Askham – Gamston

Distance: 5 to 6 miles (Roads, fair path)

Map: O.S. Pathfinder 763 (Clumber Park and East Markham)

Start: Rockley bus-stop. (Grid reference SK 716747)

Access: East Midlands bus 36 or 34, Retford – New Ollerton, roughly hourly with connections to Nottingham. Part of Sherwood Forester Network. Car drivers can make the route circular with an extra mile of road walking, limited parking at Rockley, Gamston or Askham that are to be found off the A638 road.

The Duke William (0777 83564)

A quiet village local of character and charm; the landlord has deeds going back to the 1820s. The pleasant bar contains a collection of Iron Lasts and old coins in the beams, while the interestingly shaped lounge contains various bric-a-brac. Whitbread Trophy is served on hand-pump, and a selection of bar meals is available. The pub is open from noon until 3pm at lunchtimes and from 7pm in the evening on Mondays to Saturdays. Sundays usual hours. Please note that children are not allowed in the bar but the two seats outside are good sun traps.

Askham

An attractive little village without any outstanding features but not without interest. The church of St. Nicholas has work from the 13th to 15th century, but it is the wooden gateway for King George V's silver jubilee that catches the eye with its elegance and dignity.

The Walk

(1) From the bus stop follow the lane past the old almshouses in Rockley towards West Drayton and the Run of the Mill Restaurant. After passing the impressive Rockley House (1826) take the covered walkway past the restaurant, with the attractive pond to your right. Go through 3 gateways and cross a footbridge over the River Idle, where in one night in 1826 over 800 pounds of eels were caught after a thunderstorm. Follow the path across the field and footbridge to the compact St Pauls Church, which is the beginning of West Drayton Avenue that leads to Clumber Park. St Pauls has a Norman doorway but was locked.

Retrace your steps to Rockley, cross the main road carefully and take Holme Lane for the 1.5 miles to Askham.

(2) At the T-Junction turn left to the Duke William, and then cross the road to look at the church. From the church turn left, carry on down the road out of the village, and 150 metres after the end-of-speed-restriction signs turn left up a gravel road by a metal footpath signpost.

(3) To your left is a small stream-cum-ditch; keep this to your left for the next mile. Ignore the turnings left to the house and farm, and follow the intermittent yellow markers as the road degenerates into a grassy track. Eventually you come to a field; follow this on its left-hand side by a nettle-ridden bank above the ditch. You are aiming between the farm and the house in front of you, keeping the hedgerow on your left. When this turns right, follow it for 10 yards before turning left through a gap in it by a yellow waymarker. Keep to the left of the field and pass through the orchard of the house to the right. Continue along the track from the house towards the road, keeping an eye out for giant fungi up to 21" in diameter in some waste ground by the wood.

(4) At the road turn left past Gamston Wood, owned by Notts Wildlife Trust and open to members only. Details of membership, including guides and maps to their large number of sites throughout the county, can be obtained from 310 Sneinton Dale, Nottingham NG3 7DN. On the right we meet Eaton Wood which is open to the public, and if time permits is well worth a stroll. As the road turns right go left down the dead end lane that skirts Gamston Wood. Extensive views over the

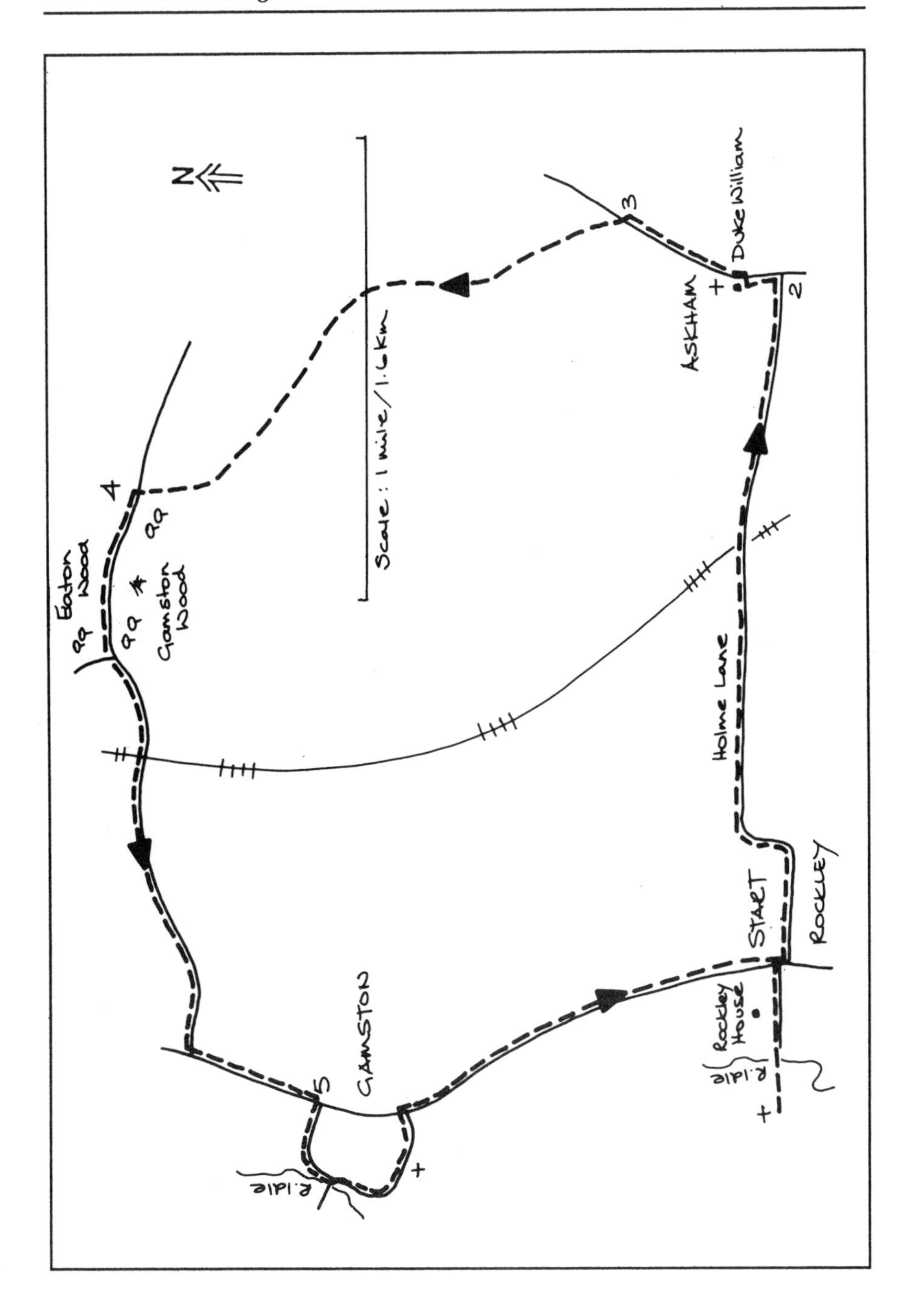
N
Scale : 1 mile / 1.6 Km
Duke William
ASKHAM
3
2
4
Eaton Wood
Gamston Wood
Holme Lane
START
ROCKLEY
Rockley House
R. Idle
GAMSTON
5
R. Idle

Sherwood Forest area are had as you drop down to the stiles over the busy railway. Keep to the lane until the main road is reached, turning left to the bus stops.

(5) Again if time allows, a walk around Gamston is pleasant. Turn right up Rectory Lane on the Ollerton road, carrying straight on as the main road turns right over the Idle. Follow the road as it curves left towards the church with its odd turret and battlements. The seat in the lane outside is a very pleasant place to sit if the bus is not yet due; otherwise carry on down to the main road and turn left to the bus stops or right to Rockley for your car.

The Duke William

26. CLUMBER PARK

Route: Duncanwood Lodge – South Lodge – Clumber Bridge – Hardwick – Elkesley

Distance: 7.5 miles. (Good paths, old roads)

Map: O.S. Pathfinder 763 (Clumber Park and East Markham)

Start: Duncanwood Lodge, near Budby, on the B6005 (Grid reference SK 613716)

Access: East Midlands 33, Nottingham – Worksop, passes the lodge. There is no bus stop visible but drivers will drop you nearby if you ask them. East Midlands 34, Retford – Ollerton, connections to Nottingham via the 36 and 33, serves Elkesley. Part of the Sherwood Forester Network. Car drivers can construct circular walks from either end, using the Dukeries Tavern as the pit stop. Travel on the A614 from Nottingham.

The Robin Hood, Elkesley (0777 83529)

A village pub, serving Boddington's and Whitbread Trophy beers which are quaffable. A locals' public bar is often lively and the lounge is quite pleasant. Open 11am -11am on Saturday, but closed from 3.00pm – 5.30pm in the week. Usual Sunday hours. The outside tables are a good place to wait for the bus, and the menu a range of snacks to full meals. Families are welcome.

Dukeries Tavern (part of Clumber Park Hotel)

Formerly the Normanton Inn, this recently extended pub is distinctly up-market, catering mainly for the car-driving family. It is open 11-11, Monday to Saturday. Usual Sunday hours. It has outside tables and a playground, and it is the only pub in the vicinity. It serves Boddington's Bitter and Marston's Pedigree. By no means is it a local, but it is there to serve the thirsty rambler.

Clumber Park

Now owned by the National Trust, it is one of the most visited sites in the country and a beautifully landscaped park. Over 130 species of birds have been noted here, and there are delightful walks through the many quiet areas of its 3700 acres. The house of 1770, built for the Dukes of Newcastle who owned Clumber, was pulled down in 1938. Its contents were sold to pay death duties, but its site is marked by paving stones in front of the surviving stables. The lake was constructed from 1778-1798, and the Chapel is considered among the finest examples of Victorian Gothic Revival architecture, dating from 1889.

Although the sheer number of visitors can make it less than pleasant at times, they can be avoided by walking along lesser used paths. One feature of the park not included in this walk is the 2.2 mile long Lime Tree Avenue, said to be the finest in Europe.

The Walk

(1) Take the bridlepath opposite Duncanwood Lodge that passes to the left-hand side of the picnic area. A Robin Hood Waymarker indicates the route, and we continue past a gate on the well-used path. Continue for 800 metres, with young birch to your left, and on meeting a fork take the left-hand signposted path; effectively carrying straight on, with a Robin Hood sign some 70 metres later.

(2) At South Lodge, built in 1824, turn left through the imposing iron gates flanked by greyhounds and continue up the tarmac road to Clumber Bridge. A variety of handsome trees and the lack of other walkers make this section a delight to linger over. Pause on the bridge for the view of the Chapel, and then turn right down some steps onto a meandering path that follows close by the lake to the site of the old house. The shop in the stables carries an excellent selection of local interest books, and the information room at the back will give advice to birdwatchers on what is around and where.

(3) Carry on to the Chapel and admire Bodley's well-balanced design. On leaving turn right and right again along the path to the North of the

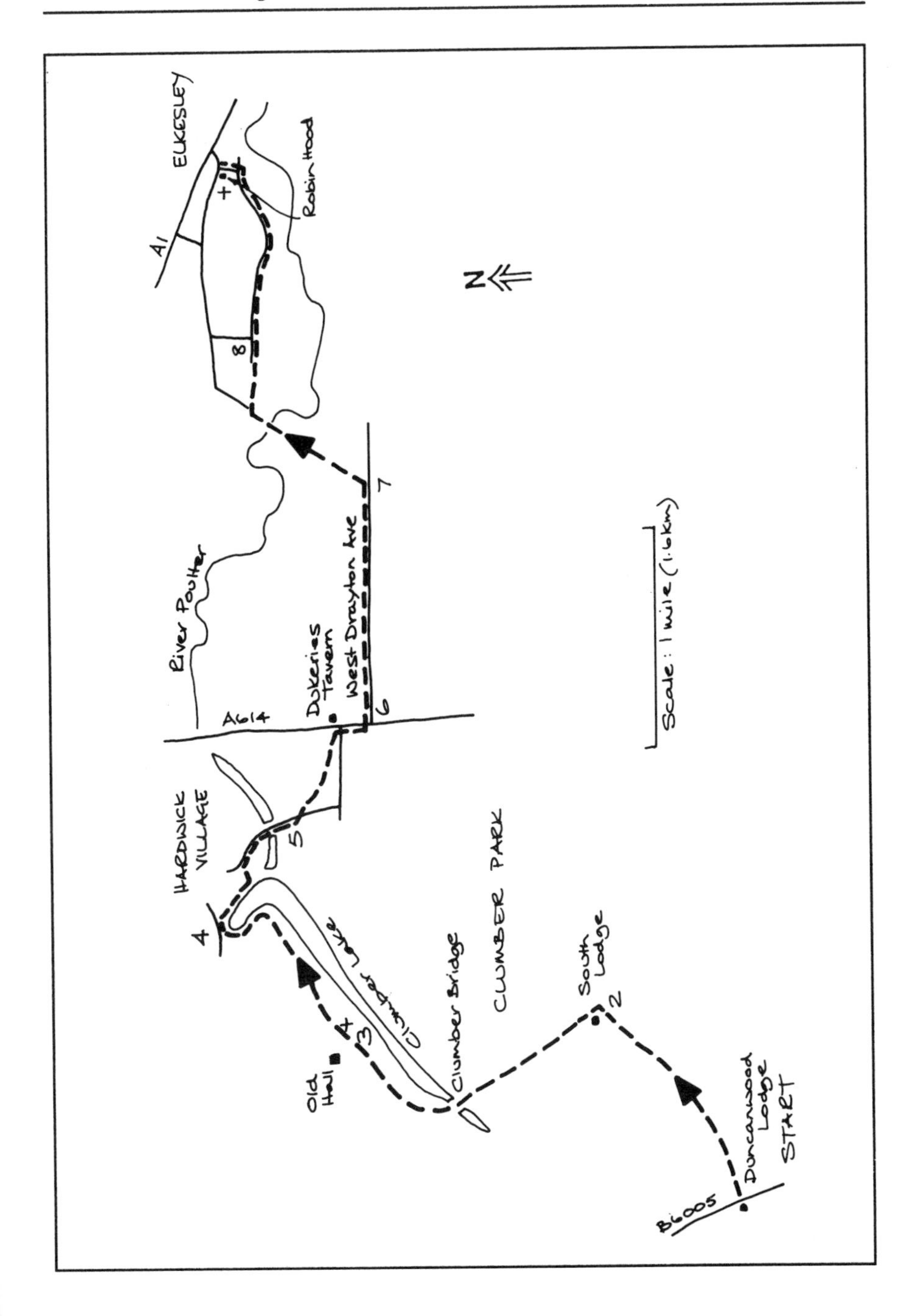
ELKESLEY
Robin Hood
A1
8
N
River Poulter
Dukeries Tavern
West Drayton Ave
7
6
A614
HARDWICK VILLAGE
5
4
CLUMBER PARK
Clumber Lake
Clumber Bridge
South Lodge
2
Old Hall
3
Duncanwood Lodge
START
B6005
Scale: 1 mile (1.6km)

chapel. The path passes a small kiosk of bus shelter proportions, and weaves through towering Cedars and Hornbeams, the latter home to Hawfinches. Just after the path curves to the right, turn left at a crossroads and go through a stone archway and gate. Cross the field, and at the next gate follow the Robin Hood waymarker and the path by the fence to the right. Keep to the edge of the wood, turning left at the lake inlet, and then go right along the embankment path that separates two smaller ponds from the main lake.

(4) Go onto the road and then quickly turn right along the edge of the lake. As you come to Hardwick Village turn left up a dirt track after the Portaloos, which were there at the time of the authors' visit, with the farm on your right. Then, turn right and right again around the farm onto the main road. The village was built in the 1770s for the estate workers to live in, which is why, as in Budby, there is no pub. Go down the road to the ford, an excellent site for bird-watching. Passage waders may be seen in the flooded marsh to the right, whilst the reed beds to the left attract hobbies after the roosting swallows.

(5) Continue along the road for 50 metres after the ford, and then turn left through an open gateway by a low wooden sign with BW and an arrow carved on it. This points the way diagonally across the field on a noticeable path, emerging through a gate onto a road. Turn left, go through the gateway and into the Dukeries Tavern which is to the left of the hotel. On leaving turn left, and after 100 yards of traffic, turn left up West Drayton Avenue by a footpath and Robin Hood marker. This is opposite one of the main Clumber entrances, and was originally built as a private driveway for the Dukes to access West Drayton church.

(6) Keep straight on for 40 metres, and as the main track turns left continue on the path past a very old gate, then onto a red gravel drive. When this drive goes right, continue on the path by the waymarkers to rejoin the road further on. Continue straight on, ignore a left turn and follow the farm track which then becomes a road. To your right the odd collection of buildings and tanks is Bothamstall Oil Field, one of several in Nottinghamshire.

(7) After 400 metres turn left to follow a line of telegraph poles along a bridlepath in a cornfield, the first pole having a blue waymarker attached. Go between the trees and then take the gravel road that goes to

the left of straight ahead, down to the ford. Cross the bridge over the River Poulter, from which Clumber Lake was formed, and turn right at the first road and familiar green outlaw. At the woodyard entrance turn left between the fence and a hedge onto a footpath, which then joins a small road.

(8) Go down the road for 600 metres, turning right at the T-Junction into Brough Lane. Follow the lane as it bends slightly to the left in an arc, and then as you reach the old part of the village, turn left to the Robin Hood. The bus stops are at the pub, and there is a timetable on the wall.

27. RHODESIA (WORKSOP)

Route: Rhodesia – Chesterfield Canal – Lady Lee – Shireoaks – Netherthorpe – Turnerwood – Chesterfield Canal – Shireoaks – Rhodesia.

Distance: 6 miles

Map: O.S. Pathfinder map 762 Worksop South and Staveley, and Landranger 120 Mansfield, Worksop.

Start: Woodhouse Inn, Rhodesia (Grid Reference 566804)

Access: There is a daily train service to Shireoaks from Sheffield and Worksop. Daily bus service from Sheffield and Worksop. By car – travel on the A57 from Sheffield, to the end of the dual carriageway section of the Worksop Bypass. From Chesterfield or Mansfield you will approach on the A60. Either way, at the roundabout, take the road signed to Town Centre, then first left. The Woodhouse Inn is three-quarters of a mile away, just beyond the junction signed to Rhodesia. There is parking on the right, just beyond the pub in the lane marked as a No Through Road, before you get to the flyover.

The Woodhouse Inn, Rhodesia (0909 274727)

The Woodhouse Inn is a welcoming hostelry offering cask Bass and a grand pint of Stones. It is open from noon until 3pm and then re-opens at 7pm on Mondays to Saturdays. Usual Sunday hours. Families are welcome and there is an outdoor area.

Worksop is the gateway to the Dukeries from the north. It is also a market town of character nestled around the fine medieval church. The Chesterfield Canal passes through the town offering a green lung into the countryside.

The Walk

(1) From the Woodhouse Inn, cross the main road and proceed down the lane by the side of Rhodesia Post Office. At the end of the row of cottages, the road crosses the remains of the Chesterfield Canal. Unfortunately the bridge has now gone and the canal is culverted. No matter, the towpath route still exists, so go left, cross another road and pick up the towpath on the south (right) side of the canal. This first section is dominated by the new Worksop Bypass, which strides across the canal and the adjacent settlement with a classic disregard for the resultant noise and visual effects. At least the engineers of this road have left sufficient headroom for navigation when the canal is restored. Come to think of it, they have left sufficient headroom for a Chesterfield Canal sailing boat to come through under full sail!

(2) Despite the nearness of the A57 on the right, and a local road on the left, this stretch of canal is surprisingly rural and peaceful. Soon the first lock is reached, unfortunately no longer useable, though there are proposals for a restoration of the entire canal, with the Worksop to Rhodesia stretch high on the agenda. Carry on along the towpath, passing under the traditional arched bridge and then under the new bridge that carries a link road up to the Bypass.

(3) Just beyond the new bridge, there is a further bridge on your right and at right angles to the canal. This marks the start of the erstwhile Lady Lee branch canal. A quick trip to the top of the bridge will give a good view to the tower of St Annes church, but will reveal that all trace of the canal has vanished. When the adjacent field has just been ploughed, the canal line shows up as different coloured soil. A signpost directs you across the field to a flight of steps leading up the embankment and onto the Bypass. The footpath at this point follows the line of the former towpath and is difficult to negotiate, especially when the field has been ploughed. If you don't fancy muddy boots, you can cheat as the author did, and use the adjacent road instead!

(4) On reaching the bypass, cross with care at the tarmac area provided, and go down the far side of the embankment on the steps, to reach fields again. There is still no sign of the erstwhile canal, though the map shows the footpath to be in the field to the left. However, what evidence there

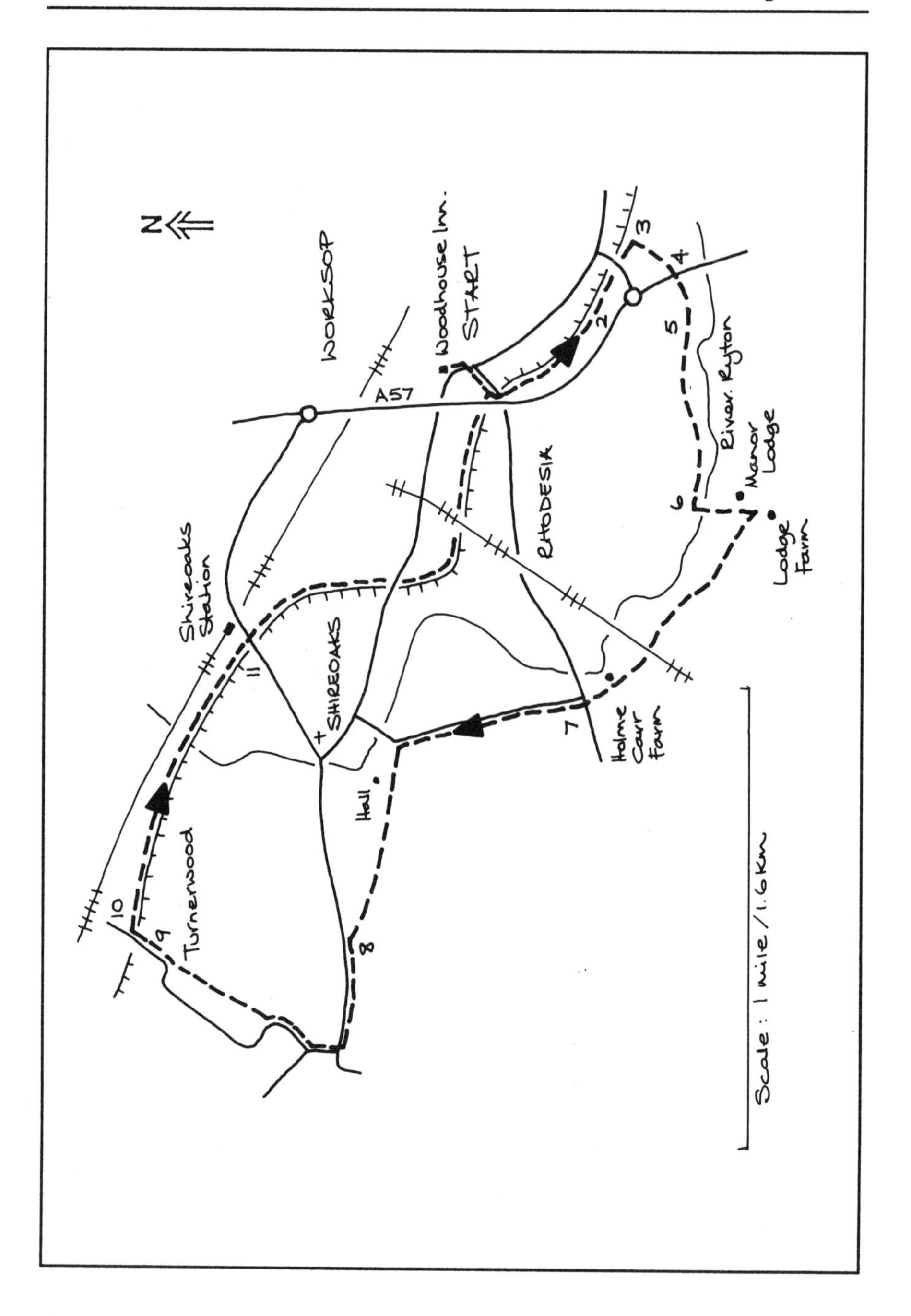
N
WORKSOP
Woodhouse Inn.
START
A57
RHODESIA
River Ryton
Manor Lodge
Lodge Farm
Holme Carr Farm
SHIREOAKS
Shireoaks Station
Hall
Turnerwood
2
3
4
5
6
7
8
9
10
11
Scale : 1 mile / 1.6 Km

is of use of this path, indicates that most people don't attempt to follow the old towpath line, which wanders through the middle of the field. Instead they seem to go through the broken fence at the bottom of the steps and follow the line of the hedge. The going is easier on the right-hand side of the hedge, though the canal seems to have been on the opposite side.

(5) Keep by the hedge to the end of the field where there is a gap. Pass through the gap onto a more obvious path and go left, into the field that once held the canal. The path leads away to the right here and enters the trees. Here there is a surprise, for after a couple of small plank bridges the canal is encountered, still in water! There are glimpses to the left to Manor Lodge, a fine-looking building though somewhat run-down. The path runs between the canal on the right and the River Ryton on the left, to the point where the branch finished. Here you turn left along the track towards Lodge Farm.

(6) The track soon crosses the river and then another bridge of a similar design to the one seen at the start of the Lady Lee branch. However, this is not another canal, but the bed of a mill leat. Go past the new house and then through the gate on the right, which takes you onto a well defined track in the fields. The track soon comes alongside the mill leat again. Here it looks even more like a canal. Continue along the track, which passes underneath the Mansfield Worksop railway line and soon reaches Holme Carr Farm. Skirt round the left of the buildings and follow the farm access down to the road. If time is pressing or if it is pouring with rain, a right turn here, along the road, will soon bring you back to Rhodesia.

(7) If you are continuing with the walk, go straight on, down the road signed to Shireoaks. There is neither footway nor much verge on this road, but it is lightly trafficked and it makes for fast walking. Ignore the first footpath sign on the left and continue along the road, in the direction of the village which is seen ahead. At the second footpath sign, by the 30 mph sign, go left through the gate and head along the driveway towards the white house. Just before the house, keep left, through a gate and so enter the grounds of Shireoaks Hall. The path is waymarked along a terrace fronting the hall and separated from it by what was once a formal garden and a "ha-ha". A "ha-ha" is the name given to the ditch and wall that you will see on your right. Its purpose

was to keep animals from straying into the formal gardens, while still allowing the residents of the Hall an uninterrupted view down the garden and into the parkland beyond. The hall is in a sorry state and the garden and parkland must once have been magnificent. It is still very attractive. At the stile by the gate, the path crosses the main vista from the Hall. To the left is the semi formal avenue, with the long "canal" feature beside it. To the right is the main frontage of the Hall itself. Cross the vista and bear right towards the pond, leaving the "canal" to your left. As you near the pond, now extensively used for fishing, turn left and head towards the gate in the hedge. There is no stile, but the gate opens and lets you out into fields again.

There is no obvious path in this next field, but head straight across towards the tall trees seen on the far horizon. A stile will then be found in the hedge, but the path beyond is even more indistinct than before. There is an uncomfortable feeling that you are not wanted, for every so often small aeroplanes fly overhead, very low and very slow. Fear not, for they are more interested in landing safely at the nearby Netherthorpe airfield. This soon comes into view ahead as you continue to make for the two tall trees. There is a stile in the fence in the far right-hand corner of the field, by the sheep pens. If the field is ploughed, as it was when the author reconnoitred this walk, it is easier to go right, along the field edge, then left at the fence and follow this along to the stile. The field on the right is use for a variety of motor sports, so, what with the planes and the sport, this could be a noisy section of the walk.

(8) At the stile, head across the next field to the gate, which brings you out onto the road. Here go left and walk along the road to Netherthorpe. At the first junction, by the farm, go right, (signed to Kiveton Park). Almost at once, go right again, this time taking the lane signed to Turnerwood. The lane soon bends left and here there is a footpath sign on the right and a clear path across the fields, heading towards the clump of trees on the horizon. The path is easily followed as it rises gently and then bears right to a gap in the hedge to the right of a wooden building. This is the hamlet of Tunerwood. Go straight on to the road and there turn right, NOT into the works, but winding past the cottages to the bridge over the canal. This is the main line of the Chesterfield Canal and the walk from here on needs very little in the way of explanation. If you were very foolish, you could do it with your

eyes shut. However you would miss the most delightful part of the walk and there would be a fair chance that you would end in the canal.

(9) On the left of the bridge are the remains of two locks, for this section of the Chesterfield was heavily locked, the climb up from Worksop to the tunnel mouth at Kiveton required 31 locks. This part of the canal now owes its existence to the fact that it is used to supply water to the still navigable section east of Worksop. There are long term proposals to restore this section and a grand bit of canal it will be too. Go right, just beyond the bridge, and descend to the towpath by the short wider part of the canal. This is a typical feature of the Chesterfield Canal. Between most of the locks on the main climbs to the tunnel there is a wider stretch. This not only allowed boats to moor or pass, it also acted as a small reservoir. Most of the locks on the eastern side of Turnerwood are single, but those to the west, and those west of the tunnel at Norwood flight, are in pairs, threes and fours.

(10) Proceed along the towpath, admiring the views, the wildlife and the industrial archaeology. Try and count the locks, but don't go too close to the edge. All the locks are "weired", which means that the gates have been removed or replaced by permanent blocks, so that the water cascades over them like a waterfall. There are occasional glimpses of Shireoaks church on the right and then the canal passes over the River Ryton on a three-arched aqueduct. Soon the canal comes out of its fringing trees as Shireoaks station is approached. The canal keeps close company with the railway through much of its length, partly because the canal route was the obvious one to pick, but partly because the canal company and the railway company were very closely intertwined. Indeed, the Chesterfield Canal company converted itself into a railway company in an attempt to forestall railway competition, and it was not until the 1950's that commercial carrying finally ceased on the lower part of the canal.

(11) At Shireoaks station the canal line is blocked by a culvert so the towpath rises to road level by the Station Inn. Public transport users will join/leave the walk at this point. On the opposite side of the blockage, the towpath resumes and a path slants down from the pub car park to join it. A short distance along the towpath the route swings left and rises to cross a bridge. This took the towpath over the Shireoaks Colliery branch canal. The remains of the pit and the canal basin are to the left.

Coal was still carried from here by canal until the end of the second world war. The railway bridge is the next feature, carrying the Worksop to Mansfield line over the canal. Then the new bypass begins to intrude on the senses.

(12) Pass underneath the viaduct carrying the A57, and at the final weired and culverted lock, turn left along the road, past the post office to reach the Woodhouse Inn.

The Woodhouse Inn

28. RETFORD TO WORKSOP (along the Chesterfield Canal)

Route: Retford railway station – West Retford – Ranby – Osberton – Manton – Worksop railway station

Distance: 11 miles (add 600 metres for the diversion to the pub in Ranby; add 1400 metres for the diversion to Scrofton, giving a total walk length of 12 miles,)

Map: O.S. Pathfinders 745 (East Retford North and Blyth) and 762 (Worksop South and Staveley)

Start: Worksop Station GR.585797

Access: Public transport is required for this walk, as it entails a train journey from Worksop to Retford. There is a daily service to Worksop from Sheffield, Retford and points in Lincolnshire. There are connections at Retford and Sheffield from much further afield – it would even be possible to do this walk on a day trip from London! There are also good bus services to Worksop from the Mansfield area.

If travelling by car, follow the A57 to the junction with A60 then follow the signs to Carlton. At the junction with the B6045, go right, towards the town centre and then right again just over the level crossing into the car park. Parking at the station is free to rail passengers.

The Chequers Inn, Ranby (0777 703329)

There is a dearth of pubs on this walk, apart from those in the towns at either end. The only accessible pub is the Chequers Inn at Ranby, a haven mid-way along the route. This free house sells a range of beers including Boddingtons, Castle Eden and Marstons Pedigree. Food is also served every day. The pub fronts the canal and has an attractive beer garden sloping down to the water. The drawback is that it is on the opposite side of the canal to the towpath, so that to reach it involves a road walk! The Chequers is open all day Mondays to Saturdays and children are welcome in the restaurant only. Usual Sunday opening.

The Station, Worksop

The Walk

(1) The walk begins with a train ride to Retford from Worksop. This takes about 10 – 15 minutes and a single fare is about £1.40 (in 1993). Worksop station is a superb survival. Built by the Manchester Sheffield and Lincolnshire Railway in the 1840s, it is constructed of local stone in a mock Jacobean style. The modern booking office facilities have been very tastefully added and the whole place is a credit to the local BR staff.

At Retford station, the first task is to find your way out. The train from Worksop arrives at the low level platforms and you make your way onto the high level platforms that serve the East Coast main line from Kings Cross to Edinburgh. Follow the Way Out signs through the soapy coloured brick buildings onto the road outside.

(2) Go across the station approach and down Victoria Street, turning left by the old Co-op, now the Retford Heating and Plumbing Supplies. Continue along this road until it reaches a junction opposite the

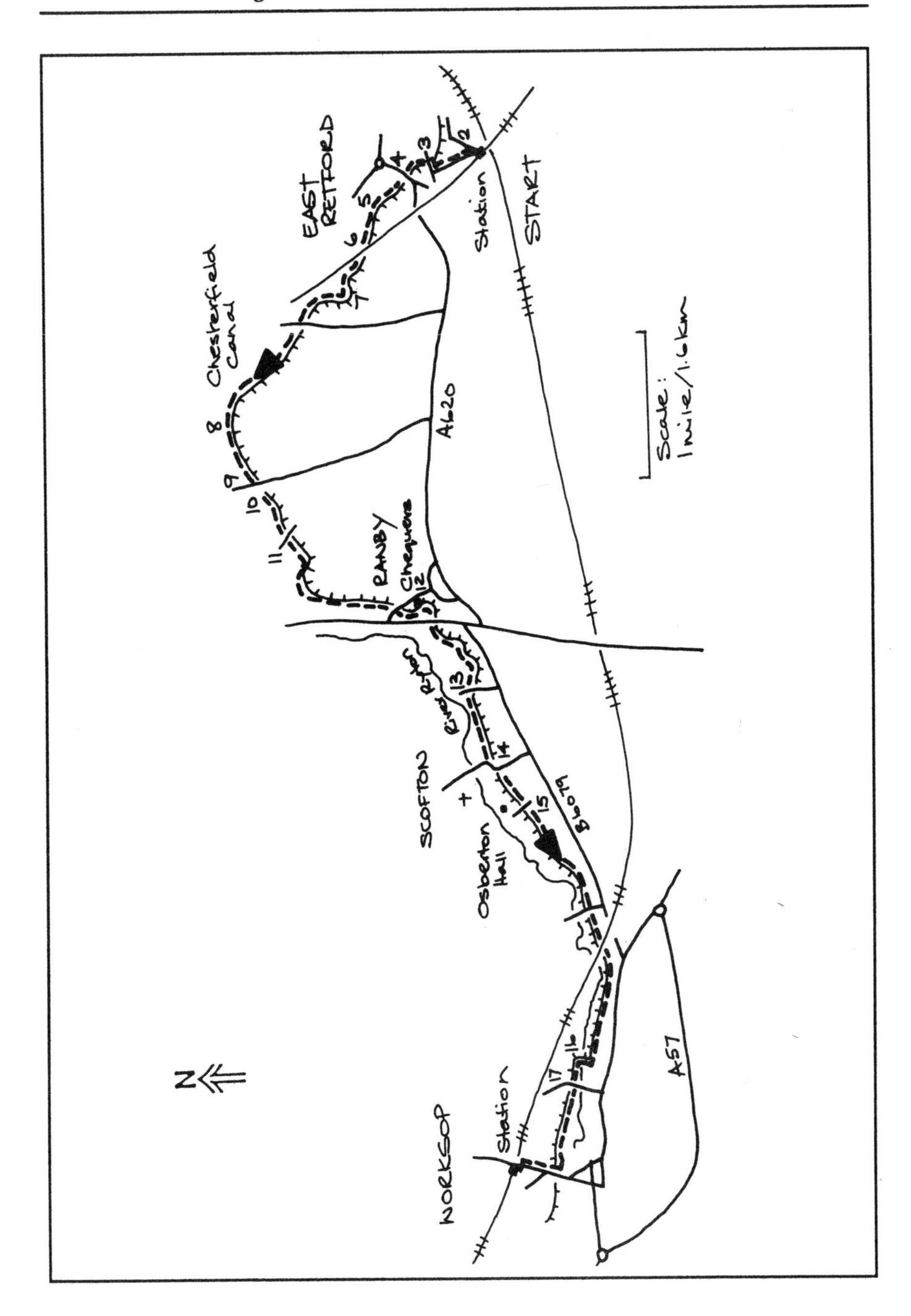
EAST RETFORD
Station
START
Chesterfield Canal
A620
Scale: 1 mile/1.6km
RANBY
Chequers
River Ryton
SCOFTON
Osberton Hall
B6079
A57
WORKSOP
Station
N

Northern Inn. This is a Tetley House, but it's much too early to be stopping for a jar yet. Continue along the road and just past the pub there is the first glimpse of the canal on your right. At the T junction by the corner shop, go right, cross over the canal bridge and descend to the towpath. At the towpath go right again, to pass underneath the bridge you have just crossed. Now begins the walk proper.

(3) Despite the proximity of the town, this is a surprisingly rural stretch of canal, fringed by trees. Rounding the first left-hand bend, you come face to face with the first lock. This is still a working canal, so all the paraphernalia of locks are on display, the two types of gate, the bywash weir, the paddle gear, the huge balance beams. If you are very lucky there may be a boat coming through, but the canal is sadly underused and in the entire walk the author only saw one boat moving in 5 hours.

(4) Pass underneath Bridge 55 which carries the A620 over the canal. Just beyond the bridge is a "winding" hole on the left, where boats could turn round. The Chesterfield Canal was very much a law unto itself. It was one of the very early canals, being built between 1771 and 1777. It perpetuated an ancient route from the Derbyshire ore and coalfields to the navigable waters of the River Trent. Because it was such an early canal and because of its isolated position, only being accessible via the tidal Trent, it had its own peculiar boat "gauge" of 6'11". The boats themselves were unusual, more like miniature Humber keels than the traditional narrow boat and capable of operating in tidal waters under sail.

(5) Still tree-lined, the canal passes a cemetery on the left then goes under the ornate bridge 54A. The bridge numbering is from the Chesterfield end and the addition of a letter after the number indicates that the structure was built after the numbering had taken place. This practice is still followed on railways and canals throughout the country.

(6) Soon the overhead wires of the East Coast Main line come into view and the canal passes underneath the railway and thus finally leaves the houses behind. It is a sad reflection on our modern society that most of the houses that adjoin the canal seem to use the towpath as a dump for garden refuse. Very few seem to treat the canal bank as a resource to be tended.

(7) The canal now runs out onto an embankment with quite wide views. This is an especially good vantage point for watching the trains on the ECML. It is also good for birdlife, with heron, moorhen and many ducks on the canal itself and pheasant, partridge and many other land birds in the adjoining fields. Continue along the towpath, taking care to step round the occasional fisherman and so reach bridge 54 with its little car park. You will see very few other walkers on the canal bank, but it is well used by fishermen, most of whom seem very friendly and ready for a chat. On the stretch between bridge 54 and the next lock, keep a sharp look-out for the resident kingfisher. Often you'll just see a blur of blue.

(8) The next lock is very isolated and has no lock keeper's house. This is Forest Low Lock. Beyond the lock the canal is again on embankment and there are wide views, including a vista to the Trent power stations. Shortly afterwards, Forest Low Middle Lock is reached and then the canal passes Barnby Fox Covert, a small woodland, specifically planted for fox hunting, on the right. Moored boats signal your arrival at Forest Lock and here the towpath takes on the dimensions of a track until bridge 53 is reached, when the narrow path resumes.

(9) Just before the bridge there are some curious signs which proclaim that the "Fishery is affected by overhead power lines". Enquiries to fishermen elicited a variety of reasons for these, ranging from the danger of using carbon rods near power lines, to the supposed effects of electro magnetic fields on the shoaling habits of fish!

(10) Continue on the towpath under the bridge, noting the house on the left with a delightful garden stretching right down to the water's edge. The canal does a sharp left- and right-hand turn at this point, then heads off through fields again. Another lock is soon reached. This is the willow shaded Forest Top Lock. A dull buzzing noise can soon be heard and this steadily gets louder as the A1 is approached. Unlike a railway, the noise from a major trunk road or motorway is almost constant and it can be heard over great distances.

(11) Bridge 52 is reached and passed and then on the right there is a curious strip of woodland, very narrow, but almost like heathland, with a sandy soil and pine, oak, beech and chestnut beautifully intermingled. The canal now swings south, with only a very narrow strip dividing it from the A1. The area on your right is shown on the map as The

Barracks, but you'll look in vain for signs of a military presence. There is a bungalow on the canal bank and soon an access track runs away to the right, to a white gate. Do not go this way, but continue alongside the canal. There have been recent bank protection works here, with steel sheeting driven into the canal bed to stop the bank being eroded by the wash from passing boats. The clay "puddle" bed of the canal can clearly be seen at several points along this walk and particularly on this stretch. Soon the first houses of Ranby are reached on the right. Don't panic at the sight of a notice proclaiming that this is Wormwood Scrubs, but keep straight on to bridge 51. Go under the bridge and then, if you are visiting the Chequers, go right, up the track by the house and so reach the road. Go right here, along the road for a couple of hundred yards, to the pub. When you have finished, retrace your steps back onto the towpath at bridge 51.

(12) Continue on the towpath, past the Chequers, and then round the pronounced right-hand bend to the inelegant concrete bridge (50A), which carries the A1 over the canal. At least under the bridge it is quiet, but what a pity that the artistry that the canal designers brought to even the most mundane bridges, has been so completely lost in modern road bridge building. A structure that is to carry a principal traffic artery – be it canal, railway or road – should be designed to be attractive. After all, it is likely to be around for 50 to 100 years, (200 in the case of this canal). Just beyond the A1 is a "winding" hole of magnificent proportions. This is kingfisher territory again. Away to the right can be seen the tower of Scofton church.

(13) Bridge 50 is an original canal structure but it has a distinctly worn appearance and is held to shape by tie rods. The lane that it carries leads to Osberton Mill Farm, which is on the right.

Despite the proximity of the B6079 on the left, there is little sense of being close to a main road, and soon the lovely Osberton Lock is reached. Just before the lock, the bywash weir runs in on the right and the towpath crosses it on a bridge. There is another fishermen's car park here, and then bridge 49 is reached. The towpath goes under the bridge and then rises up beside the lock. The lock keeper's house is straight ahead. It stands on an island, with the canal on one side and the bywash on the other, an unusual arrangement. Bridge 49 is a "roving" or "turnover" bridge, designed to carry the tow path from one side of the canal to the other without the horse having to be unhitched from the boat. As you go up by the side of the lock, the towpath continues away to the right in a tight curve onto the bridge. If you are not going to visit Scofton, continue over the bridge and through the stile on the right to regain the towpath on the opposite side of the lock.

(14) If you are visiting Scofton, turn left when you reach the lane. Go down the tree-lined road which gives a good view to the left to Osberton Hall. Cross the River Ryton on the bridge, rather than attempting the ford. The church which you saw earlier is now close by on your left, but separated from the village. Scofton turns out to be a classic estate village, with all the buildings being of the same type and vintage, bar one, which looks a lot older and is built in stone rather than brick. To reach the church, go left at the sign post and follow the track to the metal gates. The church is a surprise. From a distance it looks like a well-preserved Norman building, with round window arches and other typical features. On closer acquaintance it soon becomes obvious that it is relatively modern and the date of 1833 is in the stone work. The church stands on a little peninsula of land pushed out into Osberton Park, but separated from it by a "ha-ha". Beyond the church lies the formal park, with its lake and view to the hall. Having had a good look round, retrace your steps to Osberton Lock, cross over the bridge and rejoin the towpath on the south side of the canal.

(15) This next stretch is very secluded, probably deliberately so as it passes very close to the hall. The canal passes underneath the main access drive to the hall at bridge 48. A further occupation bridge then follows, beyond which there is a view back to the hall and the canal comes out into the open again. The branches on the trees threaten to sweep you into the cut if you don't look where you are going, but apart from that there is no problem. Soon bridge 46 is reached, by an area of woodland. This bridge is also of the turnover variety and the towpath crosse over to resume its course on the opposite side of the canal. The headgear of Manton Colliery can now be seen ahead and the canal is crossed by the railway viaduct. The viaduct has obviously suffered from its proximity to the coal mine and has had to be strengthened by metal tie bars. Not the most attractive of structures! Bridge 45 follows soon after. This is a traditional canal bridge but it marks the change from a rural walk to one in what might best be described as urban countryside. Rough fields intersperse between factories and other buildings, but for

all that, the canal is still attractive and there is a pleasant dearth of rubbish in the water.

(16) Kilton Low lock is soon reached and a feeder flows in on the right from the River Ryton. This section is a popular place with fishermen and there are more walkers in evidence, though they are more of the short distance strollers, or locals using the towpath as a convenient and pleasant route. The canal swings right to cross the Ryton on an aqueduct. Note the impressive pump house, now derelict, on the left. A left turn reveals the towers of the Worksop Priory ahead and then the canal passes underneath a new concrete bridge. Just beyond is a traditional brick-arched bridge, number 44, and a lock. This is Kilton Top or Bracebridge lock. Bridge 44 is another roving bridge, so pass over it and pick up the towpath on the south side of the canal.

(17) This final section of the walk is wholly urban, with buildings crowding the canal on both sides. The towpath is well-used, but again it is surprisingly litter free, as is the canal itself. It is a credit to Worksop. Just beyond bridge 43, the towpath runs alongside a road, separated from it by a verge and railings. Ahead is the fine warehouse which straddles the canal and enabled goods to be transhipped without worrying about weather conditions. The warehouse is being restored and access to this stretch of the towpath is not possible at present. So, at the wall surrounding the warehouse complex, go left, up the steps, onto the road, nearly opposite the Canal Tavern, a Whitbread house. Go right, along the road, into Church Walk and then right again at the main road. This crosses over the canal and there is a good view of the warehouse and its adjacent buildings. On the other side of the bridge is Town Lock, which is the last working lock on the canal.

Carry on along the main road to the traffic lights, deviating only to sample the delights of the Kings Head. A short walk up Carlton Road brings you back to the level crossing and the station.

29. LOUND

Route: Lound – Hayton – Clayworth – Lound

Distance: 7.5 miles. (Dirt roads, good paths)

Map: O.S. Pathfinder 745 (East Retford North and Blyth)

Start: Blue Bell, Lound. (Grid reference SK 692860)

Access: East Midlands 27B, Retford – Bawtry, part of the Sunday Sherwood Forester Network. Travel on the A638 road north of Worksop to Lound. Car parking is possible in the village.

The Blue Bell, Lound (0777 818317)

A friendly pub converted from a Victorian House, serving an excellent pint of Boddington's. Most unusually it boasts a Petanque court, a French game similar to bowls, except that the balls are thrown onto a sandy rink. The Blue Bell opens from noon until 3pm and from 7pm in the evenings on Mondays to Saturdays. Usual Sunday opening times.

Lound

Lound is an attractive village, linked to nearby Sutton as Sutton-cum-Lound on the signposts. There are no outstanding features in the village itself, but there is plenty to interest birdwatchers with the nearby Wetlands Wildfowl Reserve and the local gravel pits. A pair of binoculars is a useful accessory for this walk.

The Walk

(1) From the Blue Bell turn left, and then left again up Chainbridge Lane. As you pass the gravel works the tarmac gives way to a dirt road, but it is still used by cars to the Watersports centre and on to Hayton itself. Continue down the road with its plentiful birdlife in both hedgerow and reservoir, crossing the River Idle by the bridge, (2). There is no marked

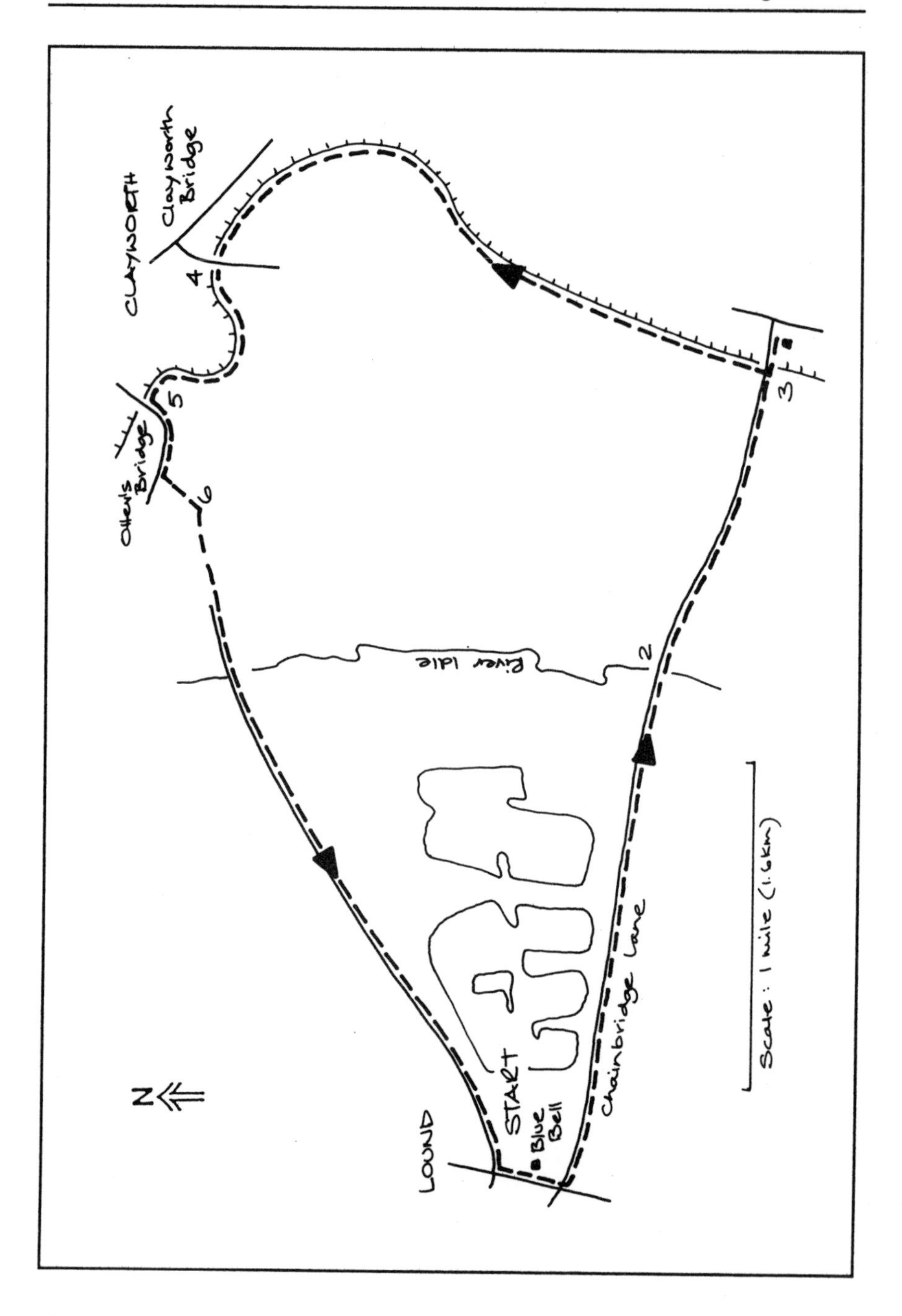
CLAYWORTH
Clayworth Bridge
4
5
Otter's Bridge
6
3
2
River Idle
Chainbridge Lane
Scale : 1 mile (1.6km)
START
Blue Bell
LOUND
N

right of way along the river bank but it seems to be used as a path for vehicles and anglers.

At the main road continue straight ahead, cross the canal bridge and turn right into the Boat Inn. This busy pub serves a good variety of meals and has Stones and Castle Eden on hand-pump. The garden has many tables and children's slides, but beware of the piped musak.

(3) Recross the canal and turn right along the well maintained towpath. After a mile a road joins on the far side, and shortly afterwards you encounter the Retford and Worksop Boat Club headquarters by Clayworth Bridge.

(4) If thirsty you can take the road from here into Clayworth; see the Gringley walk (walk 30) for descriptions of the pubs. Otherwise continue along the towpath to the next bridge, 68, with good views of the rebuilt Manor to the right.

(5) Turn left down the dirt road, and then right at the nearby junction. After 200 metres turn left over a stile by a wooden signpost, and follow the track by the hedge.

(6) At the end of the hedge the recognised right of way goes half right, aiming for a scarcely visible bridge about halfway along the woodland. However, the battered waymarker indicates that instead you should turn right along the field edge, whose hedgerow has now disappeared, turning left as you meet the large ditch at the end. This irrigation drain contained, on our last visit, a pair of kingfishers among other birds. Turn right over the well-worn bridge, aiming straight on to a large blue cross and footpath signpost. Again continue straight on following the partially overgrown bridlepath, passing a barrier to emerge by the bridge over the Idle.

(7) Follow the dirt road past the gravel pits, teeming with pochard and tufted duck in Winter, and continue until you meet the road at Lound. Turn left to the bus stop, or better still to the Blue Bell.

30. GRINGLEY ON THE HILL

Route: Gringley – Drakeholes – Wiseton – Clayworth – Gringley

Distance: 8.5 miles (Canal towpath, old tracks, quiet roads)

Map: O.S. Pathfinder 745 (East Retford North and Blyth)

Start: The Blue Bell Inn, High Street, Gringley (Grid Reference: SK 736907)

Access: Gringley is on the A631 Gainsborough to Bawtry Road. There is a bus from Gainsborough or Retford and it is also accessible by the Sherwood Forester Network. The route is circular and therefore can be started from any point; the choice of pub may influence this. Car drivers will find easy parking in Gringley, Clayworth and Drakeholes.

The Blue Bell, Gringley (0777 817406)

Although recently renovated, this pub retains its character and charm.

The Bass and Stones bitter slip down very nicely, and the food (sandwiches and pie and peas) complements the excellence of the beer. There is often a guest beer available too. The Blue Bell is open from 6.30pm on weekday evenings, noon until 3pm on Fridays and Saturdays. Usual Sunday hours.

The Brewers Arms, Clayworth.

This free house served Boddingtons and Castle Eden when we visited. A new beer garden under mature trees was very pleasant in the sunshine, and they open all day on Saturday.

The Blacksmiths Arms – visited on page 162!

Gringley on the Hill

This conservation village of 650 people is beautifully situated and contains many old brick houses constructed from the products of the old brickworks by the canal. It perches on a ridge with excellent views to the north, and it is a delight to wander about the old streets. There is an old butter cross at the west end of the High Street. To the east is the viewpoint of Beacon Hill, where Prince Rupert is said to have camped before marching on to relieve Newark during the Civil War.

The Walk

(1) From the Blue Bell, turn left towards Beacon Hill, keeping to the higher road. Pass the village hall, and when you come to a main road go straight across, up the steps slightly to the left and through the white gate to Beacon Hill. It is not known whether this is man-made or natural, despite several archaeological digs, but it does have a magnificent view for an 82 feet high hill. Lincoln can be seen on a clear day, and there is an extensive panorama in virtually every direction. From the top, which was used on Armada '88 as one of the sites for the bonfire chain that stretched throughout the country, retrace your steps through the gate. After noting the large metal beacon basket and coat of arms to the left, turn right down the 1 in 8 hill. 20 metres after passing Hillside on your left, a careful search will reveal a stile, hidden among the hawthorns, which you cross.

Follow the yellow arrows, aiming half right across the field to another stile. Cross the small nylon fence with care, and head straight ahead to a small gate to the right of the farm. Go through it, cross an old grass driveway to a second gate, and then aim half left across the field to the gate left of the brick barn, near an old trough. There, a yellow waymarker shows the direction to take across the farmyard to the road. Turn left past some interesting brick buildings, with Appleton House Farm especially pleasing to the eye.

Turn right by the post box at the next road, and take the first left up Low Street, noting how the modern buildings have been skilfully designed to blend in with the old. At the next road junction turn right by a wooden footpath sign next to Ryecroft, crossing a stile. Follow an overgrown track past a corrugated iron shed, turn left along the edge of some gardens and exit over a stile into a field. Head across the field, aiming for the large Ash tree, cross a stile and an overgrown footbridge to emerge at the road. Turn right, and after 600 metres cross the bridge over the Chesterfield Canal by Gringley Lock.

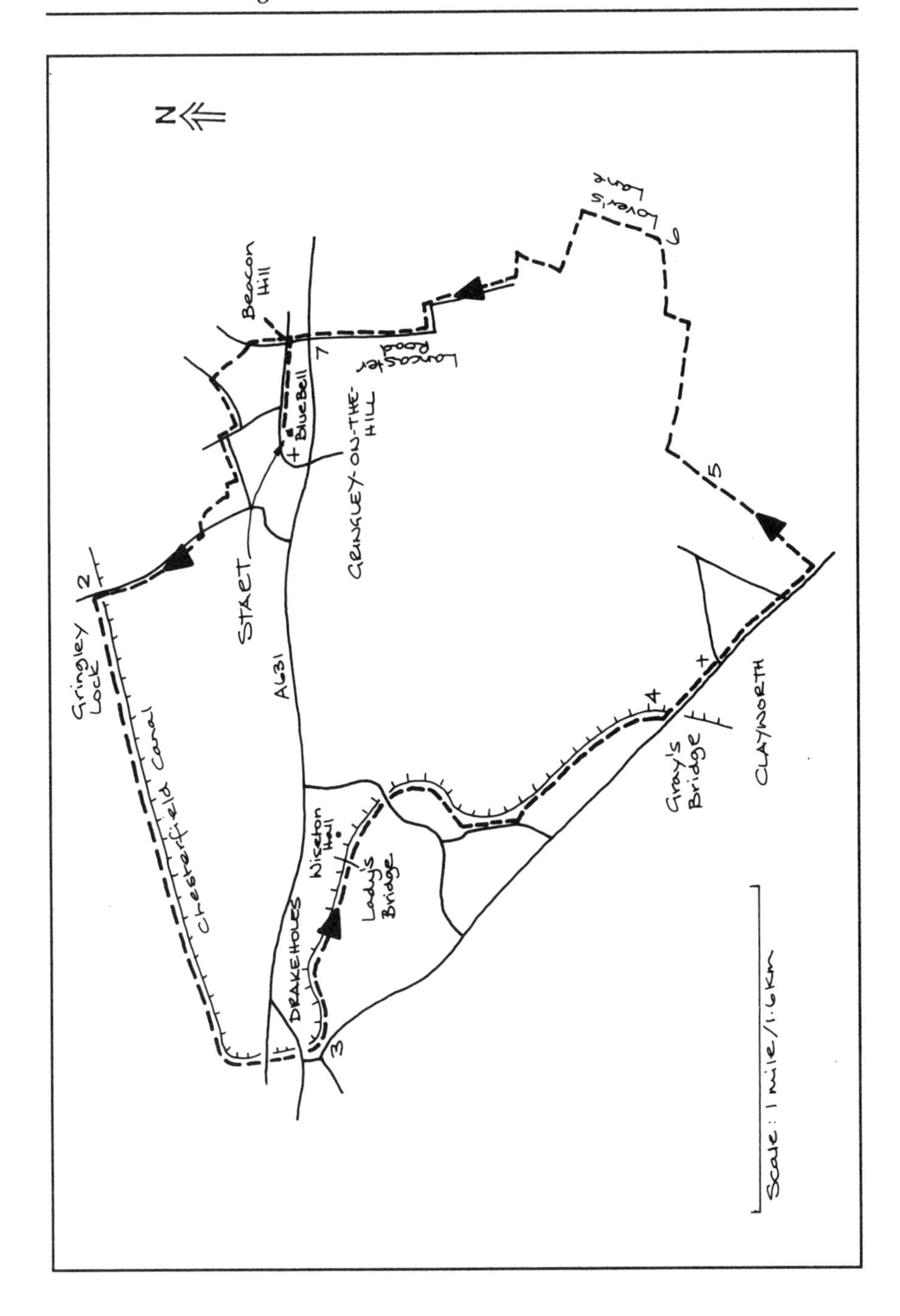
N
Beacon Hill
Lover's Lane
Lancaster Road
Blue Bell
GRINGLEY-ON-THE-HILL
START
Gringley Lock
Chesterfield Canal
A631
Wiseton Hall
Lady's Bridge
DRAKEHOLES
Gray's Bridge
CLAYWORTH
Scale: 1 mile/1.6Km
2
3
4
5
6
7

(2) Go down steps on the right to the towpath, then go right under the bridge and pass the lock-keeper's cottage. The towpath is a well-maintained grassy walkway, with a good variety of wild flowers and insects. To the left woods house a variety of warblers in summer, and the canal also attracts water birds, including a Common Tern on our last visit. To the right the farmlands stretch out for miles, making for a delightful walk.

After 1.5 miles a sharp left-hand bend takes you under the A 631 and then a slight rise leads to the top of Drakeholes Tunnel. The Griffin is passed on the right, beautifully situated, with its outdoor tables looking down upon the Chesterfield canal. A notice asks walkers to remove boots before entry to the bar where Boddingtons and Castle Eden are served by hand-pump. A separate carvery attracts families, and they do a wide range of bar meals. After a suitable break head down to the canal below where a pair of picnic tables offer a good place for eating sandwiches.

(3) Follow the well-used towpath as the canal bends back upon itself. This eccentric behaviour is to avoid the need for locks; these would have been very time-consuming for the commercial traffic for which the canal was built. Go under the elaborate Lady's Bridge which connects Wiseton Hall and Gardens. At the next bridge a diversion through the interesting village of Wiseton can be made, but since it has no pub you may prefer to carry on alongside the canal. The path joins a minor road for 200 metres before returning to the waterside. Climb stone steps just before Gray's Bridge (No. 69), and turn left over it and into Clayworth.

(4) Proceed past the church to the Blacksmith's Arms for a breather. This is a pleasant, well-kept pub with character, now offering accommodation. The regular Bass, Stones and Castle Eden beers were supplemented by Keystone Bitter on our visit, and there are two outside tables and a good selection of food.

Continue down the road to the Brewers Arms. If the weather is inclement or time is pressing, a return to Gringley by the minor road just before the Brewers can be made. However, it is much more interesting to turn left from the Brewers and after 80 yards turn left again at Beck House by the bus shelter. Ignore the metal footpath sign, although it does give an easier route via Mill Lane and Hanging Lane, because the path next to Toft Dyke is superior if more difficult. Pass a breeze-block garage and continue up the grassy lane between old hedgerows of hawthorn, elder and wild roses, which is well-used but overgrown.

(5) After a turning and stile to the left, the track becomes difficult and nettled; a stout stick or machete is useful in Summer. Press on because this path deserves to be walked, and the more people do, the better it will become. Turn right as a barbed wire fence is reached through a waymarked stile and old iron gate. Keep a hedge and electric fence to your left, walking between hawthorns on an old lane. Those to the right are oddly clumped, like a group of tepees. Go through a gate, along a wheat field and between hawthorns before emerging at a blue waymark. On the map the bridlepath heads straight ahead, but locals follow the farmer's diversion to the left up a tractor path. Turn right by the yellow arrow alongside a row of Silver Birches, cross a stile by a double yellow arrow and proceed between the widely spaced hedges. After 80 metres, a post on the left shows a blue Trent Valley Way marker, and we turn left to follow it.

(6) This is Lovers Lane, a delightful hawthorn-fringed track that meanders among the trees. The alternative route by Hanging Lane joins here. Again this is overgrown in parts but offers no problems, and we leave it over a small bridge. Turn left along the edge of a barley and then a rape field, turning right just before the hawthorn hedge. Follow the hedge as it bends left at a waymarker, joining a farm track through a gate. This is Lancaster Road, and emerges at the dual carriageway near Beacon Hill. The view on the way of Gringley, with its old sail-less windmill on the left, is most pleasing as it hugs the skyline. Cross the A 631 and continue up Green Road, turning left to the Bluebell down the High Street.